HOLY WEEK

HOLY WEEK

INTERPRETING THE LESSONS OF THE CHURCH YEAR

BONNIE THURSTON

PROCLAMATION 5
SERIES C

FORTRESS PRESS MINNEAPOLIS

PROCLAMATION

PROCLAMATION 5
Interpreting the Lessons of the Church Year
Series C, Holy Week

Cover and interior design: Spangler Design Team

Library of Congress Cataloging-in-Publication Data
(Revised for volume C, 2)

Proclamation 5.

Contents: ser. A. [1] Advent/Christmas / Mark Allan Powell — [2] Epiphany / Pheme Perkins — [etc.] — ser. C. [2] Epiphany / Gail R. O'Day.
1. Bible—Homiletical use. 2. Bible—Liturgical lessons, English. I. Perkins, Pheme.
BS534.5.P765 1994 251 92-22973
ISBN 0-8006-4193-0 (ser. C, Advent-Christmas)
ISBN 0-8006-4194-9 (ser. C, Epiphany)
ISBN 0-8006-4195-7 (ser. C, Lent)
ISBN 0-8006-4196-5 (ser. C, Holy Week)

The paper used in this publication meets the minimum requirements of American National Standard for Information Sciences—Permanence of Paper for Printed Library Materials, ANSI Z329.48-1984. ∞™

Manufactured in the U.S.A. AF 1-4196

98 97 96 95 94 1 2 3 4 5 6 7 8 9 10

To Fr. James A. O'Brien, S.J.,
and to the memory of
Fr. Daniel J. O'Hanlon, S.J.,
whose ministries have brought many to Easter

CONTENTS

Preface

The events remembered during Holy Week are at once the most joyous and solemn of the Christian year. In planning the sermons and homilies for the week the preacher will do well to think in terms of the whole sequence of events and how they are related. If sermons are planned individually the effect will be disjointed and episodic rather than that of a momentum building toward and inevitably culminating in Easter. It would be wise to read through all the appointed texts before writing any of the sermons or meditations for the week.

It is important to bring modern disciples as vividly as possible into the events and scenes of the passion of Jesus, because they are not just "once upon a time" but continuing actions with contemporary relevance. As Jean Corbon so aptly noted, "the events in which we are involved happen once, but never once for all. . . . The resurrection of Jesus is not in the past, for if it were Jesus would not have conquered our death. . . . The hour on which the desire of Jesus was focused 'has come and we are in it' forever; the event that is the cross and resurrection does not pass away" (Jean Corbon, *The Wellspring of Worship* [New York: Paulist Press, 1988], 33).

Inevitably the preacher will face difficulties with Holy Week texts. First they are familiar, so they need to be seen with fresh eyes and preached with renewed enthusiasm each year. Second, the weight of responsibility of such preaching and the depth of the mysteries addressed will be daunting to the deeply spiritual homilist. These difficulties are best faced on one's knees! Third there is an unfortunate tendency to slip into anti-Semitism during Holy Week (this in spite of the fact that recent research has pointed to the Romans as responsible for Jesus' execution). Any hint of anti-Semitism is to be avoided at all costs. In fact, the juxtaposition of Passover and Easter provides fine opportunities for Christian education, ecumenical worship, and mutual understanding.

Finally, there is the difficulty of the hermeneutical task itself. Preachers and homilists must make the events of the passion "present tense" while maintaining the textual and historic integrity of the texts and of the incidents and ideas they present. In this regard, it is always wise to do one's homework first. That is, before announcing the application to the modern situation or the connection to the contemporary hearer, the preacher should place the text in its context, and so far as possible understand its message from its author to its first audience. It is my fervent hope that the material in this slim volume will help with this task.

For those who wish to go beyond textual studies and to consider the spirituality of the Holy Week texts, two recent volumes will be of special value. St. Vladimir's Seminary Press published an anonymous work, *The Year of Grace of the Lord* (Crestwood, N.Y.: St. Vladimir's Press, 1980), which was intended to help the faithful of Orthodoxy know the calendar of their rite. The devotional and pastoral presentation of the scriptural material in the book is of immense value to all Christians, but especially to preachers. Second, Thomas Keating's *The Mystery of Christ* (Boston: Amity House, 1987) presents the liturgy, and especially the scriptural texts appointed for the various days, as spiritual experience. Another nontechnical work, this book will help the reader see beyond the surface details of events to what is really happening in the timeless realm that we share with those who were present in Jerusalem during that first Holy Week and with all the saints who have been challenged, encouraged, and ultimately redeemed by it.

It is my prayer for all who proclaim and hear these texts in 1995 that we may be brought to share in the drama and mystery of Our Lord's passion, that our hearts may be sanctified to live again in the events and scenes of his passion, and by that means, we may renew our vows to live out God's will in our day.

Acknowledgments

I am in many ways indebted to my colleagues at Wheeling Jesuit College, but especially for granting me a sabbatical year in 1993. This book was written in the spring of that year while I was Visiting Scholar at St. George's College in Jerusalem. My best wishes and thanks to the entire staff there for their help and camaraderie, but especially to Dean John Peterson and Librarian Margaret Dewey, and to my friends at the Albright Institute, and to the Ecole Biblique for the use of their excellent libraries. I especially offer my humble gratitude to the many and various Christians of Jerusalem with whom I worshiped.

Thanks are also due to Barbara Neuman, Wheeling Jesuit College faculty secretary, not only for typing this manuscript but for her constant and good-humored support of all her rowdy faculty charges; to George Miller who painstakingly proofreads and gently corrects the mistakes to which I am blind in my own work; and to Timothy Staveteig and David Lott, my editors at Fortress Press.

What is helpful here is due to my excellent teachers and mentors and to my brothers and sisters in the churches who have nurtured, encouraged, and prayed for me. What is in error is my own most grievous fault.

Sunday of the Passion
Palm Sunday

Lutheran	Roman Catholic	Episcopal	Revised Common
Deut. 32:36-39	Isa. 50:4-7	Isa. 45:21-25 *or* Isa. 52:13—53:12	Isa. 50:4-9a
Phil. 2:5-11	Phil. 2:6-11	Phil. 2:5-11	Phil. 2:5-11
Luke 22:1—23:56 *or* 23:1-49	Luke 22:14—23:56 *or* 23:1-49	Luke (22:39-71) 23:1-49 (19:28-40)	Luke 22:14—23:56 *or* 23:1-49

Holy Week begins in a spirit of apparent contradiction. It opens on Palm Sunday with the recollection of Jesus' triumphal entry into Jerusalem; but it is also called Passion Sunday because the Gospel appointed for the day is always the passion text. The day brings together triumph and death.

The custom of carrying palm branches (emblems of Christ's victory over death) in procession dates at least to the fourth century in Jerusalem. (Actually, Jerusalemites probably carried the olive branches that grow there. The nearest city where palms grow naturally is Jericho, about seventeen miles away.) In A.D. 385 Etheria, a pilgrim nun, described the procession to Bethany, where the story of the raising of Lazarus was read, and followed by an afternoon procession from the Mount of Olives back to Jerusalem, where the people carried palm branches and the bishop acted the part of Jesus. The custom made its way from Jerusalem to the Gallican rite in the West.

In the Eastern churches of the Christian tradition the focus of Holy Week is somewhat different from the somber colors with which the West paints the events. The Orthodox tradition makes no pretense of not knowing the "Easter outcome." Holy Week for Orthodox believers begins the Saturday before Palm Sunday with St. Lazarus Day, the foretaste of Christ's own resurrection and the announcement of the resurrection of all believers. In Bethany itself there is a procession from the church of Mary and Martha to Lazarus's tomb, where the Greek Patriarch reminds Christians of the joyous fact of resurrection.

The problem for the preacher is to bring together the triumphal procession with palms and the Gospel passion text. The liturgy of Palm

Sunday will set the tone for the week to come as at the outset, it summarizes the meaning of the events that will follow. The "facts" are presented in the Gospel lesson and their meaning or theological interpretation can be explained from the Old Testament lessons and epistle.

FIRST LESSON: DEUTERONOMY 32:36-39; ISAIAH 45:21-25; 50:4-11; 52:13—53:12 GOD'S SOVEREIGNTY IN HUMAN EVENTS

Three themes run through the Old Testament Lessons appointed for the day: the theme of God's power to deliver, the theme of the one who suffered for loyalty to God, and the theme of God at work in apparently evil circumstances. Easy parallels may be drawn from each both to the Philippians text and the Gospel.

Deuteronomy 32:36-39 is part of the "Song of Moses" that von Rad thinks was originally independent from the text of Deuteronomy. It contrasts the faithfulness of God with the apostasy of Israel by enumerating God's acts on Israel's behalf. In this pericope, God turns to Israel in compassion. Verse 36 reminds the hearer that God's mercy comes when the people have reached their lowest point (compare this to Phil. 2:8-9). Verse 39 places the focus squarely on God as the main actor. God is sovereign in all things, even in apparent failure and disaster. This idea might provide the homiletical starting point.

All the Isaiah texts come from Deutero-Isaiah and are dated to the sixth century B.C. The author awaits Babylon's downfall and sees in Cyrus of Persia God's liberating hand. These passages demonstrate the author's preference for lawsuit language and idol parodies, and emphasize his understanding of the universalism of God's call.

Isaiah 45:21-25 opens with the trial language of which the author is so fond and emphasizes the superiority of Israel's God (vv. 22b, 23b, 24a) and God's invitation for all nations to turn to God (vv. 22a, 23b, 24b). The universalism of the invitation is noteworthy, as is the echo of v. 23b, which is heard in Phil. 2:10. The preacher may wish to call attention to the prophetic understanding of the power of the word that is reflected in v. 23 (see Hebrews 6:13-18 on the power of God's oath).

Isaiah 50:4-11 is the third of the texts designated Servant Songs. Scholars hold a variety of opinions about the identity of the servant and, indeed, whether the texts should be so designated (see C. R. North, *The Suffering Servant in Deutero-Isaiah* [London: Oxford Univ. Press, 1956]). The portion appointed, vv. 4-9a, might be approached in terms of the three gifts of God it suggests: the gift of speech (v. 4a), the gift of hearing (vv. 4b-5), and the gift of vindication (vv. 7-9a). Note that speech is a gift for the sustenance of others and that hearing is to lead to obedience. For centuries Christians have seen v. 6 as a direct allusion to Christ's passion, but it must be remembered that the figure Second Isaiah had in mind could be quite other. (Here, and in all Old Testament preaching, the expositor must decide whether to approach the texts from the perspective of Christian application or to interpret them in the context of their own times and authors.) In the trial described in vv. 7-9 God is the advocate of the one who has suffered for obedience to God. God "vindicates" (in Latin *vindicare,* both to claim and to set free), sets free, clears from censure, and upholds that one.

The fourth Servant Song, *Isa. 52:13—53:12,* can be interpreted (as can Phil. 2:6-11) as presenting the story and meaning of the life of Jesus, and, therefore, the purpose of all God's people. The passage, however, first was significant for the exiles to whom the prophet spoke. At the very least it offered them hope and assurance of a deliverer who would fulfill God's requirements and bring healing. It reminded them that suffering is frequently God's way to success and salvation and that as one looks back upon it, suffering can be a great teacher. The five strophes of the text might provide the outline for the sermon as follows: 52:12-15—God's promise to vindicate the servant (compare 50:5-9); 53:1-3—the servant's life of suffering; 53:4-6—the servant's vicarious and atoning suffering; 53:7-9—the servant's silent submission to suffering; 53:10-12—God's purpose in the servant's suffering. Note the third strophe is in first person plural; it is a communal confession that all have sinned (see Rom. 3:23). A Hasidic teaching provides an interesting gloss on 53:7. It suggests that there are three ways that deep sorrow is expressed. At the lowest level it is expressed in cries; at the second level by silence; and at the highest level sorrow is turned into song. That the servant acts on behalf of others is strongly asserted in the text (53:4, 5, 8, 10-12) and this may provide the link to the epistle and Gospel lessons.

SECOND LESSON: PHILIPPIANS 2:6-11
THE EXAMPLE OF JESUS THE CHRIST

The "Christ Hymn" in Phil. 2:6-11 has received much commentary. Among the scholarly questions raised in connection with it are whether Paul wrote or inserted an existing hymn into his text. If Paul inserted an existing hymn, did he add the phrase "even death on a cross" to v. 8? If the hymn existed in early Christian literature, was it in Aramaic before it appeared in Greek, and are its ideas Jewish or Hellenistic? Does the hymn have a bipartite or tripartite structure? That is, does it outline the life of Jesus in terms of a pattern of descent (vv. 6-8) and ascent (vv. 9-11), or does it provide the earliest statement of the three phases of his life: his preexistence (v. 6), his earthly life (vv. 7-8), and his risen life (vv. 9-11)?

However the scholarly questions are answered, the text provides for us the theological meaning of the passion of Christ. It summarizes and explains the events of Holy Week. This should not obscure the fact that the hymn is presented in the context of the very real problems that Paul saw in the church in Philippi (see Phil. 1:27-28a; 2:3, 14; 3:18-19; 4:2-3). Paul presents the life of Jesus as a pattern to be followed by all Christians (v. 5); to have a "mind" (Greek, *phroneite*) was to have a habitual attitude. Paul is calling his hearers to rise above pettiness and self-serving. He blasts "climbing" of whatever sort, and calls believers to the self-emptying service that characterized Jesus (v. 7).

Several parallels to the Isaiah texts present themselves. Verse 7 suggests the life of the servant in Isa. 52:13—53:12 (especially 53:12). Verse 10 seems to echo Isa. 45:23. Tidy connections can be made between Christ and the servant of God in Isaiah who achieves God's ends, not through self-exultation, but through service and suffering.

The preacher might stress the difference between the essential form (Greek, *morphe,* v. 6) of Christ and his appearance (Greek, *schemati,* v. 8). Things are sometimes not what they appear to be; there is always the appearance and the truth of the matter. Apparent failure (v. 8) leads to ultimate exhaltation (vv. 9-11). Or the focus might be on the earliest Christian confession in v. 11, "Jesus is Lord" (cf. 1 Cor. 12:3; Rom. 10:9; Acts 2:36), Lord of a three-layered universe consisting of the heavens, the earth, and what is under the earth. No aspect of the cosmos is beyond the saving sovereignty of Christ.

The key to understanding the passion is the voluntary self-emptying of Jesus (vv. 7-8). The reason for Christ's *kenosis,* "emptying," is that all may claim him as Lord (v. 10) and that glory can be given to God (v. 11). Paradoxically, by renouncing royal position (v. 6), it is vouchsafed to Jesus (v. 9). Inevitably, the humiliation of the cross must follow the triumphal entry of Palm Sunday if God's plan of salvation is to become a reality. Any triumphalism that rejects the reality of the cross, or abandons service and self-giving has no place in the Christian life, a life that this text suggests is called to "downward mobility."

GOSPEL: LUKE 22:1—23:56
LUKE'S ACCOUNT OF JESUS' PASSION

The Lukan account of the passion may be divided into six sections: the plot against Jesus (22:1-6); the Lord's Supper, divided into preparation (22:7-13) and Farewell Discourse (22:14-38); the prayer on the Mount of Olives (22:39-46); the arrest and betrayals (22:47-64); the trials (22:66—23:25); and the crucifixion, death, and burial (23:26-56). Throughout, one finds the special Lukan emphases that characterize the Gospel as a whole: Jesus as the One who is with and among his disciples; a focus on women; a special interest in prayer; and the death of Jesus as the martyrdom of an innocent person.

The Plot against Jesus (22:1-6) places the events that follow squarely in the context of Passover. Judas is the agent of the plot by the religious authorities who fear popular support for Jesus. His actions are part of the supreme attack of Satan (22:3, 31, 53) and, as 22:3 and 22:53 suggest, fulfill the dark foreboding of 4:13b.

In the *preparations* for the *Lord's Supper* (22:7-13), Peter and John complete arrangements apparently made beforehand by Jesus. The fulfillment of 22:13 is meant to instill confidence in the predictions that follow in the discourse. Note the "cloak and dagger" atmosphere that characterizes the proceedings. Jesus wishes to spend this time uninterrupted with his disciples (see 22:15).

What Charles Talbert has pointed out as a *Farewell Discourse* (22:14-38) is divided into the institution of the Lord's Supper, which is close to Paul's account in 1 Cor. 11:23-26 (note Luke 22:19b-20 are omitted by the Western text), exhortations to the disciples, and predictions about what is to come. Characteristic of farewell speeches in Hellenistic literature is a teacher who knows he is to die and who gathers his community for final instruction. That instruction consists of predictions of what will happen after his demise and exhortations on how his followers are to behave after his death. Note that Luke has relocated the dispute about which one was greatest to this occasion (cf. Mark 10:41-45; Matt. 20:24-28) as part of the exhortative character of the discourse. Verses 35-38 are peculiar to Luke and fit the exhortation model of a farewell discourse, but theologically are to be seen in connection with the text that follows, which emphasizes preparation to face temptation.

The Lukan account of the *Prayer on the Mount of Olives* is the shortest of the three Synoptic accounts and emphasizes Luke's stress on prayer as Jesus' "custom" (22:39). It may be that vv. 43-44 are not authentically Lukan, but reflect later traditions about the sufferings of Jesus. An ironic note is struck in the account of the arrests and betrayals of Jesus (22:47-65), as Passover, the feast of liberation, becomes the hour of darkness (22:53). The material in 22:35-38 and 49-51 might be linked for a sermon on the peacemaking of Jesus. Luke 22:63-65 can easily be tied to Isa. 50:6 and 53:5.

The other Synoptic Gospels depict *three trial scenes:* Luke presents four (22:66—23:25), perhaps to parallel the four trials of Paul in Acts. The focus on the chief priests and scribes as instigators of the proceedings against Jesus serves Luke's purpose of demonstrating to his gentile audience that Christianity offers no offense to them. Throughout, Luke is pro-Roman and anti-Sanhedrin. Pilate is shown as finding Jesus innocent, but is weak-willed in conceding to the demands of the mob. He transfers Jesus to Herod Antipas because, as a Galilean, Jesus is properly Herod's responsibility. Interestingly the Jewish ruler (Herod) is reconciled to the Gentile (Pilate) by the passion of Jesus (23:12; see Eph. 2:14b). Note that 23:17 does not appear in all the ancient manuscripts.

Luke's *Crucifixion, Death, and Burial of Jesus* (23:26-56) emphasizes both his horizontal and vertical relationships as Jesus to the very end responds to those about him (the women of Jerusalem, his tormentors, the "good thief") and commits himself in faith to God (23:46 appears only in Luke). One might wish to draw parallels between Luke 4:1-13 and 23:35-39, temptations Jesus faces to use his power for himself versus his being "obedient to the point of death" (Phil. 2:8). As we know from 22:39 ("the disciples followed him," Greek, *ekolouthesan*), Jesus' behavior is the model his disciples must follow. In Luke the "centurion's confession" (23:47) is not a christological statement as in the other Synoptics (Mark 15:39, Matt. 27:54), but another statement of Jesus' innocence. (Declarations of Jesus' innocence form a dominant thread in chap. 23; see vv. 4, 14, 15, 22, 41, 47.) The women who have followed since Galilee were "watching these things" (23:49) and "saw the tomb and how his body was laid" (23:55). They are reliable witnesses that Jesus really died, and, in seeing his body in the tomb, they establish his corporeality. Having attested to his death, they are the appropriate proclaimers of his resurrection.

The problem facing the preacher is the sheer length of the text. For homiletical purposes he or she might focus on specifically Lukan additions to the story (22:35-38; 23:2, 6-12, 27-31, 39-43), changes in order from the other evangelists, Luke's omissions, or special Lukan emphases (see above). A helpful source on the Lukan passion is Jerome Neyrey, S.J., *The Passion according to Luke* (New York: Paulist Press, 1985). Liturgically it is more appropriate to focus on the meaning of the self-giving and suffering of Jesus than to anticipate the events of the resurrection that, of course, the original followers did not expect or anticipate. Modern disciples should recall that those who sounded hosannas may also have shouted "crucify," and during this week might well be exhorted to "rise and pray that [they] may not enter into temptation" (22:46 RSV).

Monday in Holy Week

Lutheran	Roman Catholic	Episcopal	Revised Common
Isa. 42:1-9	Isa. 42:1-7	Isa. 42:1-9	Isa. 42:1-9
Heb. 9:11-15		Heb. 11:39—12:3	Heb. 9:11-15
John 12:1-11	John 12:1-11	John 12:1-11 *or* Mark 14:3-9	John 12:1-11

Although Monday, Tuesday, and Wednesday of this week are liturgically "lesser days," they have been celebrated from the fourth century. The week opens with a focus on the new thing God is doing in Jesus. "See, the former things have come to pass, and new things I now declare" (Isa. 42:9); "Christ came as a high priest of the good things that have come" (Heb. 9:11); "God had provided something better" (Heb. 11:40). The events of this week are not separate from what preceded them, but fulfill the past. They represent the fruition of seed planted long ago when God called Israel to be the covenant people. The Gospel lessons in the first three days of this week are a series of vignettes of crucial events leading up to the crucifixion, events that both foreshadow and, in retrospect, explain the awesome finale of the week.

FIRST LESSON: ISAIAH 42:1-9
THE SERVANT APPOINTED, COMMISSIONED, AND EMPOWERED

Isaiah 42:1-9 is again from Deutero-Isaiah and includes a Servant Song (see the first lesson for Passion Sunday). The Servant Song (vv. 1-4) precedes God's charge to the servant, whose purpose is explained in terms of service (vv. 5-9).

God is clearly the speaker (vv. 1-4), and the servant seems to be Israel. We must keep in mind, however, that neither the identity of the servant nor the nature of the task is entirely certain. God chooses and upholds the servant by God's spirit. Because the servant has a prophetic task, prophetic empowerment is needed. That task is to bring justice. *Mishpat* in Hebrew (like the Arabic *din*) implies justice in terms of true religion. Note that the word appears in each verse of the text, thus characterizing the servant's work.

"Uphold" (v. 1) means primarily "grasp" or "take hold of," and indicates election for a purpose. The servant works silently (v. 2, as in 53:7), perhaps by what is done rather than by what is said. In the bringing of justice the wounded and marginalized will not be harmed; the work of justice must be done with care and tenderness (v. 3). In this work the servant will not grow faint (literally "burn dimly") or be crushed (literally "be bruised") because of his empowerment by God (v. 4).

Another poem follows. It explains what God is doing through the servant (vv. 5-9). The messenger formula (v. 5) introduces God as both physical creator and giver of the spirit, certainly an allusion to Genesis 1–3. Note that in the NRSV the creation of the world is in the past tense, while the creation of human beings is in the present. God calls the servant in righteousness to be a "covenant to the people," a much-discussed phrase, and a "light to the nations." The task reaches beyond the confines of Israel. Liberation (v. 7) is certainly spiritual as well as literal in intent, as the prophet looks for liberation from Babylon. Certainly the exiles in Babylon would have seen the idols in the great Babylonian temples (v. 8), but not God's glory in them. With what joy the exiles must have heard the message of v. 9! Their time of punishment for apostasy is drawing to an end. Certainly for them the reference is to liberation by Cyrus (cf. 41:2-4). From the old way of Babylon, the new way of Persia is springing forth. (Babylonian policy was to deport conquered peoples; Persian policy was to allow subjugated nations to return to their own lands and religious practices.)

Seen in the light of Holy Week, the text speaks of God's plan in choosing one who will be the agent of liberation. That liberation is to be understood in terms of justice, and it will be carried out with great care and consideration for the wounded and oppressed. As God revealed to John, "See, I am making all things new" (Rev. 21:5).

SECOND LESSON: HEBREWS 9:11-15; 11:39—12:3
CHRIST, MEDIATOR OF A NEW COVENANT

Like the text from Isaiah, the texts from Hebrews focus on the new thing, the more perfect thing, that God is doing in the present. It is generally accepted that Hebrews is an early first-century work (perhaps before the fall of Jerusalem in A.D. 70), written to explain the relationship of the Jewish heritage to faith in Jesus the Christ, and perhaps to show the superiority of Christianity to the Judaism from which the recipients came and into which they might have been lapsing. The letter, if such it is, relies on the Midrashic method of exegesis (some think it is a Midrash on Psalm 110) and on typology, relating past objects, events, and persons to present ones. The idea is that elements in the Hebrew tradition prefigured or were a foretaste of the Christian realities. Unlike allegory that seeks to reveal hidden meanings, typology is anticipatory and must be understood in terms of historical sequence. As does Midrash, the writer of Hebrews seeks to relate his message to the needs of the worshiping community.

Hebrews 9:11-15 occurs in a section of the letter dealing with Christ's sacrifice. While seeing Christ as both priest and sacrificial victim, it compares the partiality of priestly sacrifice to the perfection of Christ's sacrifice. The "good things that have come" in v. 11 are the sacrifice made by Christ for believers. Because the sacrifice was not "made with hands" (Greek, *chairopoiatos,* a word Jewish writers used to describe idols), it was not idolatrous. Because it was "once for all," there is no need to repeat it. Because it has eternal force, it cannot be repeated. *Redemption* (v. 12, Greek, *lutposis*) is the word Paul uses for the manumission of slaves. It was the Hebrew liturgical practice to sacrifice goats for the people and calves for the High Priests. The "blood of goats and bulls" probably refers to sacrifice on the Day of Atonement. The ashes of a heifer were used to purify a priest defiled by a corpse. Both rituals make for external purity only. Ritual sacrifices may cleanse the body, but Christ's personal sacrifice cleanses the soul (v. 14). Christ's blood had to be shed in order that the elect might receive their eternal inheritance. The word *redeems* (v. 15) is the same root as redemption (v. 12) and is associated with cost, sacrifice, and liberation.

Hebrews 11:39—12:3 concludes chap. 11, which, with its catalog of faithful persons from the past, was clearly hortatory in intention and introduces chap. 12, which relates discipline and suffering to the Christian's relationship with God. Faith is communal (vv. 39-40). Salvation is social; when any member of the community is absent, the household is not complete. (*Perfect* here anticipates 12:2.) In Hebrew *better* denotes belonging to a new dispensation. The metaphor of a stadium with spectators watching a race dominates the language of

12:1-3 (witnesses, lay aside, run, race, "set before us," "grow weary or lose heart"). The figure of the believer as an athlete of virtue may come from 4 Maccabees. The importance and reality of companionship in faith across time is stressed (v. 1). Sin is viewed in general as any impediment to relationship with God, not as a specific or individual sin. The word *cross* appears only once in the letter (v. 2). The thought is similar to that of Phil. 2:6-11 (see the second lesson for Passion Sunday). The present active indicative of "has taken his seat" (Greek, *kekathiken*) indicates that Christ's enthronement is a present reality. The writer believes that consideration of Christ gives the believer strength for the journey (and this may provide the homiletical key for the day). Interestingly, "grow weary" and "lose heart" are the verbs used by Aristotle to describe a runner's collapse at the end of a race (*Rhet.* 3.9.2). Focusing on Christ (12:2-3) and laying aside what is unnecessary (12:1) allows the runner to finish the race in good form.

GOSPEL: JOHN 12:1-11
THE ANOINTING AT BETHANY

The Gospel lesson for the day presents a picture of extravagant love and dark foreboding. John 12:1-11 is actually two stories: the anointing of Jesus (vv. 1-8), and the continuing plot against him (vv. 9-11). It is instructive to compare John's account with the parallels in Mark 14:3-9, where the woman is anonymous, and in Luke 7:36-50, where she is a sinner. Here, in his own way, John unites death (vv. 3, 7) with resurrection (vv. 1, 9). Traditionally the theological meaning of the story is seen in terms of foreshadowing the burial of Jesus.

"Six days before Passover" would be the Saturday before Passover. The Sabbath must have been over, or Mary would not have been serving. Symbolically, then, this is the day of Jesus' burial. Verse 12b reminds us of the earlier and crucial account in chap. 11. Note that, under the circumstances (11:46-54), it took courage for Jesus to return to Bethany. (Today Bethany is the village of al-Azaria; the Arabic retains the name of Lazarus, who made the village famous.)

The "dinner" for Jesus was in fact a banquet (Greek, *deipnon*), the word Paul uses for the Lord's Supper (1 Cor. 11:20). Martha was in her usual role (cf. Luke 10:39-40) and, as Lazarus seems to be a guest, this may well be in Simon's house (Mark 14:3). An interesting account of the friends of Jesus in Bethany is found in J. N. Sanders, "Those

Whom Jesus Loved (John XI:5)" (*New Testament Studies* 1 [1954–55]: 29–41.)

The first part of the text focuses on Mary's extravagant act of service and love (v. 3). Notice the great sensuality of the description. In Jesus' day only the very well-to-do could afford to use perfumes and spices lavishly. Nard was especially dear, as it came from the root of a plant that grew in what is now Nepal. We are told that the "pound" (Roman *litra,* about 12 oz.) was "pure" (Greek, *pistikes,* unmixed with anything); its value was that of a worker's pay for half a year. Then (as now in that part of the world) for a woman to uncover her hair was an act of considerable immodesty, an act more in character for the sinful woman in Luke's account. The point is found in John 11:25-27; Mary has understood what she confessed there of Jesus' unique connection to life and death. It was unusual to wipe off perfume once applied. Perhaps Jesus' feet here are a symbol of his whole body. If so, John is preparing us for the footwashing in 13:5-10. Again the fragrance in the house may symbolize the Christian community or church that is made beautiful by deeds of generosity. Or it may be John's poetic way of expressing Mark's "wherever the good news is proclaimed in the whole world, what she has done will be told in remembrance of her" (Mark 14:9).

John attempts to provide a motive for Judas's actions (vv. 4-8). Judas is a tool of Satan (13:2, 27). His cupidity was also noted by Matthew (26:15). Judas's remark about giving to the poor apparently indicates his understanding of Jesus' concern for them (v. 5). Then John explains his quite different motivation (v. 6): He hoped for more money from which to pilfer. The word *keep* (v. 7) is notoriously difficult to translate and explain. The sense of the verse is, however, clearly a reference to Jesus' impending passion. Jesus alludes to Deut. 15:11: There will always be the opportunity to help the poor, but this occasion provided a unique opportunity to serve the Christ (v. 8).

The unfolding plot against Jesus, which last appeared in 11:45-53, is picked up again at 12:9-11. Jesus' celebrity has been increased by his raising of Lazarus. Because Lazarus is a living sign of the power of Jesus, he, too, is marked for death (see 11:53). "Deserting" (Greek, *upagon*) means leaving the Jewish faith (v. 11).

The preacher might note the stark contrast between the love and devotion of Mary and the fear and intrigue of the chief priests. These represent two ways of responding to Jesus. One can meet the radical love of Jesus with an extravagant return of love. Or one can meet the radical love of Jesus, which calls for the reordering of human priorities, with fear and insecurity. The chief priests fear for their positions of power and authority (cf. 11:48), but Mary, a woman at the bottom of the power scale in her world, is overjoyed by the "new world order," the message Jesus signals (cf. Luke 1:52). Lazarus reminds us that it can be dangerous to be associated with Jesus and his message. Finally, the traditional interpretation of the passage is certainly the best one. Here is the most lavish and touching picture of loving response to the earthly Jesus. It is the standard against which we measure our own response to him.

Tuesday in Holy Week

Lutheran	Roman Catholic	Episcopal	Revised Common
Isa. 49:1-6	Isa. 49:1-6	Isa. 49:1-6	Isa. 49:1-7
1 Cor. 1:18-25		1 Cor. 1:18-31	1 Cor. 1:18-31
John 12:20-36	John 13:21-33, 36-38	John 12:37-38, 42-50 *or* Mark 11:15-19	John 12:20-36

Two themes seem to dominate the lessons for the day. First, there is a focus on the extension of God's concerns to the Gentiles (see Isa. 49:6; 1 Cor. 1:18-25; John 12:20-23; Mark 11:15-17). God is calling in and drawing together those previously estranged. The inclusion of the Gentiles is one of the Messiah's tasks. Second, the texts point up the strength God provides (see Isa. 49:5; 1 Cor. 1:22-25; John 12:27-28). God will provide the wherewithal for the tasks God calls people to do. Note, too, the underlying motif of judgment in today's texts.

FIRST LESSON: ISAIAH 49:1-7
THE SERVANT'S DIALOGUE WITH GOD

The problem of determining the exact extent of the second Servant Song is reflected in the differences among the lectionary selections. Some scholars suggest it includes Isa. 49:1-7, and some break the text at v. 6. For preaching purposes, perhaps it is best seen as a dialogue divided as follows: the servant (vv. 1-2); God (v. 3); the servant (v. 4); God (vv. 5-7). Note first that the servant is reporting God's part of the dialogue. Note also the tonal similarity to the call and confessions of Jeremiah.

The servant was destined from before birth for his task. Furthermore, God named him, gave him his essential character, and adopted him. The text opens with a call to "peoples from far away," thus anticipating v. 6. The military figures of the sword and the arrow (v. 2) describe the power of the servant's word. In his prophetic calling, he is known by his "mouth," his powers of speech (cf. 42:1-4). Although some scholars view "Israel" (v. 3) as a gloss, the idea is that Israel is the servant in whom God is glorified. God needs a people so that God's glory can be made manifest (cf. Ps. 2:7).

The servant expresses his consciousness of failure, his sense of futility (v. 4). At the same time, he knows his recompense or reward is with God. The contrast is between the high calling (vv. 1-3) and its apparent results. It is not the calling or the work that exhausts, but the sense that it is accomplishing so little that discourages the servant. (Both verses 4 and 5 use the *waw* adversative, "But I," "But now.")

At this point, the God who formed the servant and gave him his first task ("that Israel might be gathered" to God), expands the scope of his calling. God honors what he is doing, by giving him more to do! The God who recompensed him (v. 4) has become his strength. (Sometimes we must attempt what we think is beyond our ability to experience the strength that God supplies.) It is not enough to call Israel to repentance (v. 6); all the nations must be called to God, "that my salvation may reach to the end of the earth." Herein is an end to the idea that Israel's duty is for her own salvation alone. She is to be a light to others. In view of Matt. 8:19-20, Christians, too, must move beyond the idea that Christian life is for personal salvation, for "being saved" alone. The dimension of extending the borders of God's kingdom must include service to others.

Beginning with a messenger formula, which may signal a new unit of text, there is the vision that eventually the powerful (kings and princes representing their people as well) will submit to God (v. 7). The one who is despised and abhorred becomes the object of worship (see Phil. 2:6-11). This happens not because of the servant, but because of the faithfulness of God who, having chosen the servant for a task, sees it to fruition. The God who chooses is the God who is faithful to the chosen.

Recall that the entire text is addressed to foreign nations (v. 1). In the dialogue God is not only dealing with the servant, but is proclaiming God's intentions toward those to whom the servant is sent. In every way the message of God's salvation is intended to be universal, "to the end of the earth."

SECOND LESSON: 1 CORINTHIANS 1:18-25
THE WORD OF THE CROSS

The Corinthian correspondence is one of Paul's best known because it addresses not only important doctrinal issues, but matters of practical import, issues of Christian worship and behavior. Paul writes 1 Corinthians in the early 50s from Ephesus (16:8) to a city that is strategically and economically one of the most important in Greece and to a church that he knew well but did not found (see Acts 18:1-18).

1 Corinthians 1:18-25 follows from Paul's disclaimer that he was not a baptizer, one who had built parties that followed him. Party slogans of the type just discussed in 1:12 allude to an overvaluing of human wisdom. Against this Paul declares the simplicity with which the cross is to be preached, because it is its own power (an important warning for every preacher, especially in Holy Week!). For Paul the preaching of the cross of Christ was fundamental. Note how carefully constructed the text is, with its rhythmic prose and parallelisms. Note, as well, that "wisdom" is used both positively and negatively in the passage, and that Paul uses terms and examples that would have meaning for both the Greeks and Jews in Corinth.

The text opens with and works on the basis of a contrast between folly and power, the lost and the saved. "The cross" (v. 18) is not the literal means of execution, but the "word of the cross," the gospel itself. The news of the cross and its reconciliation (2 Cor. 5:19) is a message of foolishness to some, but of power to others. The quotation from Isa. 29:14 or Ps. 33:10 links the first part of the passage to the discussion of foolishness and wisdom (vv. 21 and 25). God determines what is wisdom and what is folly.

There follows in v. 20 a list of those the world considered wise, philosophers ("the one who is wise"), the learned ("the scribe"), rhetoricians ("the debater"), positions that both the Jewish and Greek cultures had and esteemed. And yet in God's wisdom, God arranged that the divinity not be known by wisdom but through the "foolishness of our proclamation" (note, not foolish preaching!). Salvation comes not through human knowledge, but through faith in what is preached, that is, the cross.

The heart of Paul's message intends to bring together Jew and Greek in Christ (vv. 23-24). As the Gospel narratives demonstrate, Jews did, indeed, look for signs, visible evidence of God's power, miracles (see for example, Mark 8:11-12 or John 4:48). Greeks were attracted to philosophical systems. Both expected God to conform to their own criteria of power and wisdom. Contrasted with these Jews and Greeks are "we," those who have accepted the preaching of the cross.

On the cross "we" see God's own definition of power in the one who prayed for his enemies and entrusted his own life to God. The power of God is seen in one who suffers for others. Thus Christ crucified is both the power and wisdom of God (v. 22), for which both Jews and Greeks are looking. Verse 25 can be read as a maxim by itself. What God has done by the cross directly contradicts human ideas of wisdom and power, but it does what neither could do, that is, reconciles humanity to God.

Paul does not disparage knowledge. But knowledge does not save, as 1 Cor. 13:8d-10 will make clear. The historical revelation of Christ, his death on the cross, brings people to God. The cross is, in the words of Isaiah, "a light to the nations." For Holy Week preaching, the sermon or homily should focus clearly on the cross, "the foolishness of our proclamation" (v. 21).

GOSPEL: JOHN 12:20-38; MARK 11:15-19
JESUS AND THE GENTILES

Both of the appointed Gospel lessons, John 12:20-38 and Mark 11:15-19, show Jesus in connection with the Gentiles. And both depict him, although differently, in his role as judge. (For commentary on John 13:21-33 see the third lesson for Wednesday of Holy Week.)

John 12:20-38 follows immediately from John's account of Palm Sunday, which again mentions the effects of the raising of Lazarus and official Judaism's displeasure. Much of the theology of the "Book of Signs" is drawn together here. That section of the Gospel opened with those who came to Jesus through others (1:41, 45) and with a feast (2:2 ff.), so we have here an example of Johannine inclusion. Here, too, is John's way of dealing with the Synoptic seed parables and with the baptism, transfiguration, and Gethsemane accounts. For convenience the text may be divided as follows: the Gentiles come to Jesus (vv. 20-27); the voice from heaven speaks, (vv. 27-28); the voice is interpreted (vv. 29-36).

The Gentiles coming to Jesus follows immediately from "The world has gone after him" (12:19). The Greeks are probably proselytes or God fearers and are to be compared with the Pharisee immediately preceding in the text. Those who do not know Jesus approach him through those who do (see 1 John 1:3-4). Andrew and Philip have already been shown bringing others to Jesus (1:41, 45). Earlier in the

Gospel, people were invited to "come and see" (1:39); now the Gentiles come "to see" Jesus. To this point, Jesus has insisted his hour has not come (2:4; 7:6, 30; 8:20); now the sign that Jesus has been awaiting has arrived. "Glorified" (v. 23) alludes to Jesus' death, as the following verses explain.

The meaning of Jesus' glorification follows (vv. 24-26). The independent saying about the grain of wheat explains in almost parabolic form the mystery of life through death (v. 24). Jesus then gives the spiritual meaning of this saying and echoes Synoptic aphorisms (vv. 24, 26; cf. Matt. 10:32). In this context, "follow me" means to crucifixion and death.

Instead of the agony in the garden of the Synoptic writers, John gives us a brief account (12:27-28). Jesus understands his purpose and submits to the will of the Father, possibly alluding to Ps. 42:5 (cf. Mark 14:33-35). When Jesus submits to God's will, a voice from heaven comes as a sign of divine assurance (cf. Mark 1:11; 9:7). There is great irony in the use of "glory" here (as in 12:23). The hour of Christ's glory is the hour of his greatest pain and suffering. Past and future are united; God has been glorified through the signs Jesus did, which will culminate in the greatest sign, his resurrection.

In the meantime, John depicts again the two poles of response to what Jesus says and does: those who understand and those who don't; the person who grasps for the quick, obvious answer (thunder), and the awed heart who sees beyond the appearances (v. 29). The cosmic overtones of the events to come are introduced. This world is to be judged, and its ruler, Satan (14:30; 16:11), is to be defeated by the power of the cross described in the Corinthian text. The "lifting up," then, (v. 32) is ambivalent as it is both Jesus' crucifixion and glorification (v. 33; see 3:14; 8:28). "All people" who are here drawn to Christ are the "much fruit" of v. 24.

Again, the response of the crowd is typically Johannine. They "trip" over the "lifted up" because what Jesus says contradicts their own understanding of their Scripture. The passage closes as, in the terms of the great light and darkness motif of the Gospel, Jesus appeals to them to take advantage of the opportunities they have left. "Children of light" is a Hebrew idiom for "children of God," those who bear their father's likeness. The image appears in the Qumran documents, 1 Thess. 5:5, and Luke 16:8. With this last warning delivered, Jesus withdraws; in John's Gospel v. 36b marks the end of his public ministry. (Verses

37-43 explain the unbelief of the Jews. Notice at 12:34 that John is using their own technique.)

Mark 11:15-19 begins the second day of Holy Week by the evangelist's chronology. It breaks the story of the cursing of the fig tree, a typical Markan "sandwich" construction, and should perhaps be tied to its interpretation. The pericope focuses on the prophetic figure of Jesus and his concern for the holiness of the Temple, which is being "secularized," and for the Gentiles and removal of hindrances to their prayers.

The merchants in the Temple area (v. 15) would be those who sold animals, wine, salt, and oil for sacrifice, and the moneychangers were those who changed gentile coinage into Temple currency. (For pigeons in sacrifice, see Lev. 12:6; 14:22; 15:14, 29.) All were there for the convenience of worshipers, but they changed the atmosphere of the Temple from one of prayer to one of commerce. The Temple area had apparently become a "short cut" (v. 16), a practice forbidden by the Talmud (Babylonian Talmud, Berakot 9:5).

Jesus' words from Isa. 56:6-8 or Jer. 7:11 provide the prophetic rationale for his action, his "sign act" in cleansing the Temple area (v. 17). Rather than a place of prayer, it had become a rendezvous place for *lestai,* bandits, brigands, robbers, rogues. The only area open to Gentiles for prayer had become a bazaar, and Jesus' cleansing of this area can be seen not only as prophetic action, but as evidence of his concern for the rights and privileges of "outsiders." (This may be the point of connection to the first lesson for the day.) His action precipitated the opposition of the chief priests and scribes (the two groups making up the Sanhedrin, v. 18). Mark keeps his chronology clear (v. 19), although he does not tell us whether Jesus returned to Bethany (Matt. 21:17) or camped with the pilgrims on the Mount of Olives.

This account has troubling features. For example, why didn't the Romans or Temple police quell the disturbance if there were one? Mark's point seems to be to demonstrate the prophetic, judging character of Jesus' actions and to show his concern for the sanctity of the Temple and for the Gentiles' access to prayer.

Wednesday in Holy Week

Lutheran	Roman Catholic	Episcopal	Revised Common
Isa. 50:4-9a	Isa. 50:4-9	Isa. 50:4-9a	Isa. 50:4-9a
Rom. 5:6-11		Heb. 9:11-15, 24-28	Heb. 12:1-3
Matt. 26:14-25	Matt. 26:14-25	John 13:21-35 *or* Matt. 26:1-5, 14-25	John 13:21-32

The lessons for today provide an opportunity for self-reflection before the solemn events of the triduum. Could we give ourselves up to shame and insult, trusting in God's vindication (Isa. 50:4-9)? Can we admit that *we* are the weak and ungodly for whom Christ died (Rom. 5:6-11)? And, finally, can we ask in deep humility, "Is it I, Lord?" examining our own temptations toward greed, ambition, and pride (John 13:21-35; Matt. 26:14-25)?

FIRST LESSON: ISAIAH 50:4-9
TO SPEAK, TO HEAR, TO SUFFER, TO BE VINDICATED

Isaiah 50:4-9 has been discussed with the first lessons for Passion Sunday, so only a few suggestions will be added at this point. First, notice the number of references to organs of the body (vv. 4-7); almost all represent something beyond sheer physiology. As is usual in the Servant Songs, the servant focuses on the task as that of delivering the word, here speaking words of comfort and sustenance (see Isa. 40:1-2). To speak and to hear "as those who are taught" (v. 4) is to be wise. Both together describe the task of prophecy in Israel: to hear God and to speak God's word to the people. Notice that God has opened the ear, allowed the servant to hear (that is, to understand), and that the result of hearing is obedience (v. 5). (On the matter of hearing see the words of Jesus in Mark 4:23-24, where hearing is tied to our own tendency toward judgment.)

The servant suffered physical abuse and insult (v. 6). Perhaps in his culture, the latter is the more difficult to bear. To destroy the beard, for example, would have been the most serious kind of insult. The servant insists that in spite of insult he has been true to his task. In his world, to accept insult meant to admit that it was justified. Therefore, his acceptance is even more remarkable (v. 7). God is on the side of the abused one. In the face of abuse, God provides help and vindication. (Verses 7a and 9a repeat the theme of the unit, "the Lord God helps me.") Interestingly, *insult* and *disgraced* (vv. 6, 7) share the same root, strongly linking the two verses.

The trial language is a forceful expression of God being "on the side" of the servant (vv. 8-9). The expected answer to the rhetorical questions is "nobody" (v. 8). Although in the opponents' view the servant has already lost by accepting shame and suffering, the servant knows his opponents can mock him as much as they like because, in the final analysis, they will perish. Those who oppose the servant will eventually be subject to decay, and thus be destroyed.

How difficult it is to continue to speak words of sustenance and comfort to others in the face of one's own undeserved suffering. Yet that is the task to which God's servants are called and for which they receive God's help and vindication. The psychological difficulties and realities expressed in the passage are no less vivid today than in the time of the Babylonian exile.

SECOND LESSON: ROMANS 5:6-11
CHRIST DIED FOR THE UNGODLY

Romans is Paul's theological magnum opus written between A.D. 55 and 59 to a church he had not yet visited. Romans 5:6-11, like the epistle for Tuesday of Holy Week, is another text explaining the meaning of the cross, which now looms even larger in our spiritual consciousness of this week's events. Paul emphasizes that God has taken the initiative to deal with the sin that estranges the human community from God. Chapters 5–8 of Romans deal with the new life in the Spirit made available by Christ; 5:1 has opened a new section of the letter.

Although there are some textual problems with 5:6, it undoubtedly presents the core of the message of the early church: Christ died for the ungodly. The "weakness" here is certainly moral weakness. The phrase "at the right time" implies that the death and resurrection of Jesus were part of a plan. Paul never sees history as random, but always as progressing according to God's design.

Unwillingness to die for another (v. 7) is a truism intended to underscore the remarkable thing Christ did: It contrasts human unwillingness to die with Christ's willingness. In an historical event we see the demonstration of God's love (v. 8). The response of God to human sin (which Paul has vividly described in Romans 1–2) is to die for it. As in 3:22b-26, the vicarious and expiatory nature of Christ's death is underscored. The intimate connection between our reconciliation to God and Christ's death (v. 9) implies that we now are justified by his blood, and in the future we shall be saved. Apparently future salvation has to do with resurrection (cf. Rom. 6:5; Phil. 3:10). The parallel construction (v. 10) reinforces the idea; we are reconciled by his death and shall be saved by his life. Christians stand between the two decisive events of human history, Christ's reconciling death and his final act of cosmic salvation, the resurrection of the just.

Note how personal Paul makes the issue. While we were enemies, we were reconciled. God's initiative on our behalf is personal in nature, and the response to it is personal: rejoicing. We rejoice in God through our Lord Jesus Christ because of our reconciliation. The reconciliation here is connected to the "peace" of 5:1. The enduring quality of the Christian life is the joy (not "happiness," which is a pagan concept without place in the New Testament) we have, know, and share because of our "righted" relationship with God. We rejoice because we ourselves are the sinners for whom Christ died. Where there has been much forgiveness, there is much rejoicing (see Luke 15:11-32; 17:11-19; 19:1-9; 7:36-50; for commentary on Heb. 12:1-3 see the second lesson of Monday in Holy Week.)

GOSPEL: JOHN 13:21-35; MATTHEW 26:14-25 THE BETRAYAL OF JESUS

The Gospel lessons describe the betrayal of Jesus. It is instructive to compare the two accounts, noting that both emphasize Jesus' knowledge of "the hour" and of betrayal from within the inner circle of his friends.

John 13:21-35 follows immediately from the account of the footwashing. (Verses 34-35 anticipate the "mandatum" of Holy Thursday, and it would be liturgically more correct to reserve them for use tomorrow.) The public ministry of Jesus is over, and now Jesus is seen only with the disciples. The betrayal is predicted (vv. 21-30), and the Farewell Discourse begins (v. 31).

Note the great drama with which John draws the scene of the betrayal prediction (21-30). He refers back to the previous speech about chosenness (v. 21), shows Jesus' emotional state in light of the knowledge of betrayal by a friend (cf. 11:33), and depicts the disciples' response to Jesus' announcement (v. 22). It may be useful to imagine vv. 23-27 as an incident among the four named characters that is not shared by all the disciples. Certainly vv. 23-24 are peculiar to John. Peter asks the disciple whom Jesus loved (cf. 19:26; 20:2; 21:7, 20) to elicit more information from Jesus. Perhaps by turning his head toward the Master he could ask without being overheard by the others.

Jesus answers the request by means of a dramatic gesture that may have been intended to obscure the identity of the betrayer. To offer a morsel to a guest was a token of friendship and oriental hospitality to one specially favored by the host. The word *morsel* (*psomion*) is Greek Christianity's word for the eucharistic host. Satan has a role in the drama (v. 27; see 13:2). The term "entered him" is used of evil spirits in Mark 5:12 and Luke 8:30. Perhaps we are to see in the scene Jesus precipitating his own passion. This would continue John's picture of events as proceeding according to his will.

Even in the immediate community of disciples the two Johannine poles of response to Jesus are seen (vv. 28-29). Perhaps the disciples are perplexed because they have not heard what Peter and the disciple whom Jesus loved have heard. Even the betrayer is obedient to Jesus (vv. 27, 30). "Night" is, of course, a great Johannine symbol. To go from Jesus is to be in spiritual darkness (12:35-36). Indeed, it is a time of cosmic darkness with the next real light occurring only at 20:1.

Note the confidence with which Jesus speaks (vv. 31-35), even in full knowledge that his betrayal is under way. Textual variants of vv. 31-32 should be consulted. Again, as in 12:23-25 and 28, there is great irony in the use of *glorified.* For John, Jesus' whole passion is his glorification. Foreseeing an immediate end ("at once," v. 32; "a little longer," v. 33), Jesus speaks as father to the family gathered for Passover ("little children," v. 33). Because they cannot follow where he is going, he tells them how to keep his spirit alive among themselves.

As previously mentioned, the commandment to love one another (vv. 34-35) liturgically belongs to Holy Thursday. The theme of following Jesus' commandments occurs six or seven times in the Farewell Discourse. In the context of the passion, to love as Jesus has loved implies laying down one's life for others. Love of others is the central ethical teaching of the early church (see 1 John 2:7-11) and the mark of discipleship across the ages. The test of our discipleship is how we treat others. In the words of Teilhard de Chardin, "How we treat people is how we treat God."

Matthew 26:14-25, the account of the betrayal, immediately follows the anointing at Bethany. Judas's response is contrasted with that of the woman. The focus is entirely on the Twelve to emphasize betrayal from the inner circle. The text may be divided as follows: Judas agrees to betray Jesus (vv. 14-16); Passover preparations (vv. 17-19); and Jesus predicts his betrayal (vv. 20-25).

Matthew deals with the perennial problem of the motivation of Judas (vv. 14-16). Was he merely the tool of Satan, or was he motivated by greed or disappointed political ambitions? Was his intent to force Jesus' hand but not to betray him? We cannot know for sure. Matthew does make clear that Judas took the initiative in going to the chief priests to ask, in effect, "What is it worth to you to have Jesus betrayed?" The exchange of money was to bind Judas to the bargain and reflects Matthew's interest in the fulfillment of prophecy (Zech. 11:22). Once the arrangements are made, Judas simply awaits an opportune moment for betrayal.

Matthew's account of the preparations for Passover (vv. 17-19) is much shorter than Mark's (14:13-16). Jesus had made prior provision for the meal with unknown (to us) friends providing a place. Matthew's addition of "my time is near" (v. 18) recalls John's "the hour has come" (12:23). Some scholars think vv. 21-25 were not part of the original passion narrative, although this is difficult to explain because it has fourfold attestation.

As in John, here in Matthew, Jesus reclines with his disciples and announces that one of them will betray him (vv. 20-21). Here, however, the announcement was clearly heard by all and confusion ensues as each asks, "Surely not I, Lord?" (v. 22). The response of Jesus in v. 23 is ambiguous because presumably all who had been eating with him would have used the common dish. (Are we to conclude from both accounts that Jesus wishes to protect Judas so that he can be about his dark task?) Verse 24 indicates that, while Judas fulfills the prediction, as its agent, he is still responsible. "As it is written" reflects Matthew's interest in fulfillment of Scripture, although which text he has in mind is not clear (see, for example, Psalm 22; Isaiah 53; Zech. 13:7). The statement, "It would have been better for that one not to have been born," may be a paraphrase of 1 Enoch 38:2.

Judas calls Jesus' bluff. Unlike the other disciples who call Jesus "Lord," Judas inquires, "Surely not I, Rabbi?" perhaps already indicating his shifting loyalties. Jesus, knowing full well the answer to the question, places upon Judas full responsibility for his actions.

In the face of the momentous events of the triduum to come the question "Surely not I, Lord?" has particular rhetorical power and invites us to examine the spiritual motivations that could bring us to disaster: greed, ambition, and pride. Where do we stand in relation to Jesus who is about to wash our feet and offer his body and blood for our redemption?

Maundy Thursday

Lutheran	Roman Catholic	Episcopal	Revised Common
Jer. 31:31-34	Exod. 12:1-8, 11-14	Exod. 12:1-14a	Exod. 12:1-4 (5-10), 11-14
Heb. 10:15-39	1 Cor. 11:23-26	1 Cor. 11:23-26 (27-32)	1 Cor. 11:23-26
Luke 22:7-20	John 13:1-15	John 13:1-15 *or* Luke 22:14-30	John 13:1-17, 31b-35

In the ancient church Maundy Thursday focused on reconciliation as public penitents were received by the bishop. It was not until the fourth Century that Maundy Thursday became part of the triduum of Easter. Egeria reports that in Jerusalem the faithful met at 7 P.M. on the Eleona (Constantine's church on the Mount of Olives) for prayers and hymns until 11 P.M. when "the Lord's teachings were read." At midnight there was a procession with hymns to "the place from which the Lord ascended into heaven" where hymns and antiphons were sung until cockcrow when, at the place where Jesus prayed in the garden, the Gospel passages were read.

The fifth century calendar of Poleminus Silvius calls the day *natale calicis,* the birth of the chalice. In the Orthodox churches, however, Maundy Thursday's liturgy focuses on the footwashing. With great ceremony the bishop, archbishop, or patriarch washes the feet of his clergy. The image evoked is intended to be that of the servanthood to which Christ calls his people.

Three root events of faith are commemorated on this day: Passover, the institution of the Lord's Supper, and the footwashing. Each reflects God's initiative in responding to and dealing with human need, and thus the character of God's love. Both the Lord's Supper and the footwashing symbolically foreshadow the crucifixion and depict Jesus' giving of himself in loving service. The impending betrayal of Jesus by Judas casts a dark shadow over all the events and should be kept in mind by the homilist.

FIRST LESSON: EXODUS 12:1-14; JEREMIAH 31:31-34
GOD'S DELIVERANCE FROM SLAVERY AND SIN

Exodus 12:1-14 comes from the priestly tradition concerning Passover. The festival itself probably predates the exodus, but was given new meaning at that time. The Hellenistic period of Judaism fixed the rituals of Passover. Notice in this text that 12:15 ff. integrates Passover and the Feast of Unleavened Bread; this precedent is followed by Mark, Matthew, and Luke. The language of Passover became the language of Christian faith, especially for Paul and John, and the writer of 1 Peter 2:22 brought together the Passover lamb, the symbol of the cost of redemption, with the figure of the suffering servant. By the fourth century Christian exegesis of Passover was allegorical or typological.

Exodus 12:1 begins with a standard priestly opening formula indicating that the instructions are to be taken as directly from God. The text explains how to choose the Passover lamb (vv. 3-6); describes how to eat it (vv. 8-11); and associates the apotropaic rite with the blood of the lamb (vv. 7, 12, 13).

A postexilic community is presupposed (vv. 3-6), as the meal is a family meal with lamb as its main course. Josephus tells us that ten persons was the minimum for a "household." Because the lamb was for a holy purpose, it must be blemishless. A one-year-old male represented reproductive capacity, and thus wealth to a shepherding people (see also Lev. 22:19-25 and Deut. 15:19-23). Care is taken that food not be wasted. Verse 6 literally says the lamb must be killed "between two evenings," that is, in the afternoon before sunset (NRSV says "at twilight").

Unleavened bread (v. 8) is a symbol of the haste with which the original meal was eaten, but leaven was also symbolic of evil and corruption. The bitter herbs (probably lettuce, chicory, peppermint, snakeroot, and dandelion) symbolized the suffering of slavery. Because the roasted lamb had been sanctified or set apart, "holy," nothing of it must be left that could be used for questionable purposes (v. 10). The meal is to be eaten immediately before the journey (v. 11), in this case the journey to freedom and to covenant with God at Sinai.

Verses 12-13 are slightly at odds with v. 7, which seems to reflect a more ancient rite. From earliest records, blood has been associated with sacrifice and attributed efficacy to save. The marking of the homes of the Hebrews not only gave the deity blood, traditionally God's part of a sacrifice, but symbolized the preciousness of the life offered. It is significant that God smites not only the Egyptians, but their gods as well (v. 12), because the contests between Moses and Pharaoh that precede the exodus are really contests between the gods of Egypt and the God of Israel.

The Passover rite is to be kept "throughout your generations" (v. 14), a mark of its significance. The Hebrews are to remember a history that focuses on the mercy and deliverance of God. In recent times many Christian communities have combined seder meals with commemorations of the Last Supper. A useful resource for such events is Joseph Stallings, *Rediscovering Passover: A Complete Guide for Christians* (San Jose, Calif.: Resource Publications, 1988).

Jeremiah's ministry, which spanned the years from 627 to 580 B.C., saw the fall of the Assyrian Empire and the rise of Babylon. His oracles against Judah and Jerusalem, which called for God's people to return to God, were probably transcribed by Baruch. *Jeremiah 31:31-34* comes from what is sometimes called the "Book of Consolation," chaps. 30–31, and is probably the most familiar text by the prophet. Scholars have noted its resemblance both to Deutero-Isaiah and to Deuteronomic diction. The passage is chiastic in form; vv. 31-32 describe the old covenant in prose, and vv. 33-34 describe the new covenant in poetry. The text follows from vv. 29-30, which reflects the shift from a corporate to an individual understanding of responsibility for sin. Verse 29b was probably a popular proverb of the time.

The prophet announces that God is about to make a new covenant with the whole people ("the house of Israel and the house of Judah," cf. 11:10b). "The days are surely coming" reflects strongly eschatological language. The reference (v. 32) is both to the exodus and to the covenant at Sinai. Because *covenant* is a relational term, the reference to God as the husband of Israel is appropriate. It echoes not only the language of earlier prophets, but also, in cultural terms, that God is the senior party in the covenant. The covenant at Sinai that was broken was the moral law represented by the Decalogue.

Verse 33 uses the oldest term for covenant making, "to cut a covenant" (RSV). "After those days" refers to the days described in v. 28. God is not giving a new law, but is putting the law within them. Jeremiah often refers to the heart (3:17; 7:24; 9:14; 11:8; 13:10) understood as the corporate seat of will and intention. The sin of Judah written on the heart (17:1) is now balanced by the new law written on the heart. To "know God" is to have direct connection with God and reflects profound intimacy (see Hosea 6:6). "From the least of them to the greatest" means either from youngest to oldest or from the lowest social classes to the nobility. The sin of all people will be so completely forgiven that it will not even be remembered. Forgiveness of sin provides new incentive for keeping the law. Always behind God's forgiveness is the motivation of God's love.

This text is alluded to in reports of Jesus' institution of the Lord's Supper ("This cup is the new covenant in my blood") and is quoted in Heb. 8:8-12. A very helpful discussion of "The New Covenant" is William L. Holladay's article by that title (*Interpreter's Dictionary of the Bible,* Supplementary Volume, 623–25).

SECOND LESSON: 1 CORINTHIANS 11:23-26; HEBREWS 10:15-39
THE NEW AND LIVING WAY THROUGH HIS FLESH

1 Corinthians 11:23-26 is the oldest New Testament text on the institution of the Lord's Supper. It occurs in the midst of a long discussion of propriety in worship (11:2—14:40), and its immediate context is abuses of the Lord's Supper in Corinth (11:17-34). These abuses can be traced to factionalism (see 1:10—4:21) and to social divisions that led to the wealthy arriving first at the Supper and eating and drinking to excess so that, when the poorer Christians (many of whom may have been slaves) arrived, there was nothing left. Both factionalism and the practical result of social stratification showed lack of understanding of and reverence for the rite.

"Received" and "handed on" are technical terms for passing on tradition (v. 23). Paul undoubtedly learned the traditions of the Lord's Supper from members of the Jerusalem church, so no special revelation is implied. There is certainly direct reference to Jesus' actions and to a particular event. The structural device that Paul uses in the passage is to report what Jesus did and then to give his explanation of the action. *Bread* (v. 23) is the common word for bread or loaf, not the Greek term for matzoth. After the thanksgiving (by which the rite has come to be known), Paul reports the formula that is repeated (v. 25b). The repeated formula underlines the fact of solemn commemoration.

While there is question about whether the formula reproduces the authentic words of Jesus, the statements remind us that the table is his and not ours. It is now common knowledge that in Aramaic, the language Jesus spoke, the verb *to be* would be absent. For *is* we might substitute *means*. (To exemplify the point in German, the idea is expressed by *das heisst,* not *das ist.*)

Jesus handled the cup "in the same way" (v. 25), suggesting that he first blessed it. The formula ties the cup to the new covenant of the Jeremiah text (31:31-34). Literally understood, blood would be a great problem for the Jews, and for our interpretation. *Covenant* is the operative term here; meaning as it does "last will," it stresses God's initiative, gift, and ultimate intention for humanity.

The death is linked to the return of Jesus (v. 26). The Lord's Supper is intended to be a meal that looks back to the passion of the Lord and at the same time forward to his ultimate triumph. His death is, in fact, the beginning of his parousia and eternal kingdom. As the church enacts the Lord's Supper she is visibly crying out "Maranatha." In this context it is well to remember that proclaiming the death of Jesus is what Paul understands himself to be called to do (see 1 Cor. 1:17; 2:1-2).

Most preachers will draw the immediate parallel between the Passover and the Eucharist. Liturgically this is obvious and warranted, although one should be wary of the historical and textual difficulties involved. In both the Passover meal and the Lord's Supper it should be noted that the most powerful symbols are drawn from common aspects of daily life. When God directs us to what is most holy, God asks us to look afresh at what is around us all the time. Note that both the Passover and the Lord's Supper are meals of pilgrimage intended to fortify the recipients for their journey toward the God of Sinai and Golgotha. (For a fuller treatment of the early church's practice of the Lord's Supper see chap. four of B. Thurston, *Spiritual Life in the Early Church,* Fortress Press, 1993.)

Hebrews 10:15-39 is basically an exhortation to faithfulness (vv. 19-25 and 32-39) and a warning against falling away (vv. 26-31). It opens with a quotation of the Jeremiah text (see first lesson for Maundy Thursday) and proceeds with an image of worship in the Temple that advances the theme of Christ as High Priest of a new covenant (vv. 19-25) from the earlier part of the letter. Verses 19 and 20, with their references to the blood and flesh of Jesus, which have ushered us into the holiest places ("through the curtain"), provide the link to the institution of the Lord's Supper, which is commemorated on Maundy Thursday. Within this section are three exhortations that might provide an outline for the sermon: "approach" (v. 22, a call to devotional life); "hold fast" (v. 23, a call to attitudinal steadfastness); and "provoke," (v. 24, a call to practical activity).

The horror of intentional sin after having received Christ sounds the sharpest note of judgment in the letter (vv. 26-31). Note that the text discusses deliberate (Greek *ekoslos,* "willing or voluntary") sin, not unintentional lapses. The language of v. 29 ("spurned," from the Greek *katapareo*; literally, "to trample or stomp on, to treat with utter contempt") makes this clear. Verses 32-39 encourage faithfulness on the basis of past experience. In the past sufferings were endured with compassion and joyful acceptance. Continued confidence and endurance assure reception of "what was promised." It is on the basis of past endurance that the writer insists on the faithfulness of his audience (v. 39).

These verses are a source of spiritual encouragement to modern Christians as we journey toward Easter through the terrible events of the next forty-eight hours. We draw near to participate in these events, holding fast to faith in Jesus in spite of his apparent "failure," and stirring each other up as we consider the command (the corruption of the Latin *mandatum*) to love as we have been loved (John 13:35-36).

GOSPEL: LUKE 22:7-20; JOHN 13:1-15
JESUS' ACTS OF LOVING SERVICE

Luke 22:7-20 is that evangelist's account of the institution of the Lord's Supper. Luke uses the meal as an occasion for a farewell speech (see discussion of the Gospel for Passion Sunday). The text may be divided as follows: preparations for the meal (vv. 7-13) and the Lord's Supper (vv. 14-20); Jesus' disposition (vv. 14-16) and his acts (vv. 14-20).

Luke's account of the preparation for the meal is more like Mark's than Matthew's. Although it may not be historically correct, v. 7 serves to root the reader in time and space. Luke's Jesus sends Peter and John to prepare the meal (v. 8). The text seems to assume that Jesus spent his days somewhere other than in Jerusalem (v. 10).

For responsible exegesis, the homilist should consult the textual commentaries on vv. 14-20. The issue that the homilist must decide is whether to omit 19b-20 (which echoes 1 Cor. 11:24b-25). "When the hour came" (v. 14) clearly means evening, but is strongly symbolic. As he is portrayed throughout Luke, here, too, Jesus is "with" his disciples. Verse 15 not only predicts again his suffering, but, with the prior provision for the meal that Jesus has made, reinforces his desire to eat with the disciples. Certainly he knows his end is immanent. Luke's account has a strongly eschatological note (vv. 16, 18).

The Lukan text as recorded by the NRSV has two cups of wine. Certainly this reflects the Jewish character of the meal. There is no reason to think that early Christianity had a monolithic liturgical tradition at the end of the first century. The Lord's Supper could have been celebrated differently in different Christian communities. Stylistically, the parallelism of vv. 15-16 and vv. 17-18 lead to the material in vv. 19-38.

The preacher will certainly want to emphasize Jesus' act of self-giving as it is reflected in this text. As the Passover meal was both a sacrifice that turned away God's wrath and a sustenance for the journey ahead, so the Lord's Supper reflects Jesus' giving of himself for our redemption and remaining with us as we journey into the future that ultimately holds his return in glory.

John 13:1-15, the footwashing, opens a new section of that Gospel sometimes called the "Book of Glory." John's passion story begins not with the triumphal entry but here, where for him the church is born. The footwashing must be seen as an act of love like the institution of the Eucharist, an action symbolic of the death of Christ and his giving of himself. Synoptic parallels might include Mark 10:35-45 and Luke 22:24-27. The text may be divided as follows: the context and Jesus' knowledge and actions (vv. 1-5); the dialogue with Peter (vv. 6-11), which gives the key to the meaning of the act; and the explanation of the act (vv. 12-15), which expresses its ethical application. The keynote of the chapter is the love of Christ, which his disciples are themselves to manifest (13:1, 34-35).

The majestic figure of Jesus (vv. 1-5), who has complete foreknowledge of events and is in complete control, assumes the role of a slave. "The hour" is the subject of the Book of Glory. Jesus' destination is the Father (cf. 16:28), and he loves his own "to the end," meaning both "completely" and "to the eschaton." The footwashing follows the statement of Jesus' origin and end, both of which represent acts of humility. Jesus "got up from the table" (v. 4), so this is not the usual washing at the beginning of a meal (a service that the disciples had forgotten to perform for each other?). Jesus "laid aside his garments," which were rightly those of his lordship, and "girded himself with a towel" (v. 4 RSV), the attire worn by a human slave. "Laying aside" and "taking" is the same language John uses for the laying down of life (see 10:11, 15, 17-18). Because washing feet was a task so menial that it could not be required of a Jewish slave, one wonders how the disciples felt as their Lord stooped to perform this service.

John symbolically explains the salvific necessity for the death of Jesus (vv. 6-11). It would be helpful if we could hear the tone with which Peter asks the question "Lord, are you going to wash my feet?" (v. 6). Verse 7 is certainly to be understood as prediction. Literally "later" means after the cross and resurrection; the Farewell Discourse to follow explains that much will become clear after the resurrection. To have a "share in me" (v. 8) will also be illuminated by the discourse to follow. The point here is that Peter, and all Jesus' disciples, must trust Christ even when he does things that seem incomprehensible. Like Peter, we sometimes find the hardest task of all is to be served. (Verses 8-10 are taken by some to introduce the theme of baptism, but that certainly represents a secondary level of meaning.)

Verse 10 is probably the most difficult verse in the pericope. It is intended to help Peter see the reality behind the symbol, and depends upon our knowing the social custom by which a visitor is offered a bath after a long journey or, alternatively, a guest bathed at home before arriving at a banquet. Again Jesus has complete foreknowledge of events (vv. 10b-11).

When Jesus returns to his own garments (and his role as Lord and Teacher), he raises questions that force the disciples to think about what has happened (vv. 12-15). "Teacher and Lord" (v. 13) may well reflect the order of the disciples' understanding. Jesus accepts the titles, but he changes the order to "Lord and Teacher" (v. 14) and explains what it means to be both. We see the nature of God and the standard that nature sets for us. Verse 15 is a call for mutual willingness to serve each other. In the kingdom of God those who are "lordly" are those who voluntarily perform lowly service (see Mark 9:35; 10:43-45; Matt. 20:26-28; 23:11-12; and Luke 9:48; 22:26).

Luke 12:37 provides an interesting gloss on this text: "Blessed are those servants whom the master finds awake when he comes; truly, I say to you, he will gird himself and have them sit at table, and he will come and serve them." The act of the washing of feet became a liturgical rite only in the seventh century. In modern services it is effective only if worshipers understand that the action is symbolic of Jesus' death and his giving of himself in love.

Good Friday

Lutheran	Roman Catholic	Episcopal	Revised Common
Isa. 52:13—53:12 *or* Hosea 6:1-6	Isa. 52:13—53:12	Isa. 52:13—53:12 *or* Gen. 22:1-18	Isa. 52:13—53:12
Heb. 4:14-16; 5:7-9	Heb. 4:14-16; 5:7-9	Heb. 10:1-25	Heb. 10:16-25 *or* Heb. 4:14-16; 5:7-9
John 18:1—19:42 *or* 19:17-30	John 18:1—19:42	John (18:1-40) 19:1-37	John 18:1—19:42

The events of Maundy Thursday culminate on Good Friday. The question that the risen Lord asked Cleopas and his companion on the Emmaus road might well focus our thinking about this day: "Was it not necessary that the Messiah should suffer these things and then enter into his glory?" (Luke 24:26).

Good Friday is the "day of the cross," and in all preaching and liturgical activity for the day, the cross must be focal. Traditionally Good Friday is a day of strict fasting and abstinence. In Western liturgical churches, the altar has been stripped to symbolize mourning, and as a sign of that mourning, in the ancient church no one received communion on that day. In the third century Good Friday was known as the "Pascha of Crucifixion," and the Orthodox churches retain this nomenclature today. In Egeria's day (fourth century) the morning was taken up with reading the lessons describing the trial of Jesus, and in the afternoon, the bishop's throne was set up on Golgotha and relics of the cross were venerated, after which the texts describing Jesus' sufferings were read and "all people weep during these readings."

In the Orthodox churches today Good Friday is commemorated by a burial liturgy for the Christ. At the front of the church stands Jesus' bier, elaborately adorned with candles and flowers. As the liturgy of Christ's entombment progresses, the bier is carried in procession and the faithful venerate it and further deck it with flowers. Christ's death is thus personalized; it becomes a family funeral with the resultant atmosphere of deep emotion and mourning. Each participant is reminded that this death was for him or her.

Theologically, Good Friday confronts us with the mystery of the cross and of suffering. The texts appointed for this year speak of the hidden purposes of God that stand behind the apparent injustice of innocent suffering.

FIRST LESSON: ISAIAH 52:13—53:12
SURELY HE HAS BORNE OUR GRIEFS

Behind Isaiah 52:13—53:12 is the common idea that suffering is God's punishment of sin (see Job). While the unrighteous sufferer "gets what he deserves," the righteous sufferer has value in the community. The text contrasts suffering and humiliation with exaltation, and it is marked off by a double inclusion as it opens and closes both with the servant's triumph and with the words of God. The text may be divided for exposition in several ways. One might focus on the two speakers; God (52:13-15), the people (53:1-11a), God (53:11b-12). Traditionally the passage is divided into three-line strophes; the servant is introduced (52:13-15); the servant's life of suffering is described (53:1-3); the theme of the first strophe and the servant's vindication by God is repeated (53:10-12).

Overall, the text points to the servant's victory. The astonishment (52:14; 53:1) sets the tone for the whole passage. Note the number of verses that stress that the servant has "borne our griefs" or "bore iniquities" (53:4, 5, 6, 8, 10, 11, 12). Christians interpret these verses as the explanation of Jesus' sacrifice for others, and for centuries have understood the passage to "predict" what happened to Jesus during the passion.

Isaiah 52:13-14 introduces the text in the terms we have already seen in 42:1-4. "Disfigured" (v. 14) is probably a better translation of the Hebrew than the "marred" of the NRSV. The significance of the servant is seen in the response of kings and nations to him (v. 15). Recall that he has already been described as a light to the nations (42:6; 49:6).

Some scholars have seen behind Isa. 53:1-6 Akkadian influences and references to the Babylonian Tammuz liturgies. We must hear the incredulity behind the questions (vv. 1-3) and remember that the "arm of the LORD" is the agent of his power and salvation. Verse 2 describes the undistinguished origins of the servant in terms of scrub, desert growth (this in the context of beauty being a mark of divine blessing; cf. Jer. 23:5). Verse 3 is language descriptive of the response to a leper.

Not only is exile and solitariness a bitter punishment in Near Eastern culture, but it is considered dangerous even to look at an object of divine wrath. "Suffering" (v. 3) is literally "pains," and "infirmity" is literally "sickness."

Verses 4-6 contrast the servant and the speaker, "we" and "he." Unlike the expected response (exemplified by the friends of Job), here the sufferer is understood to bear the consequences of others' sins. His suffering is the penalty for "our" sin and the means of our reconciliation and restoration. The image of the sheep (v. 6) prepares the reader for the next strophe.

Silent submission to suffering (vv. 7-9) is not characteristic of Old Testament sufferers. Verse 8 is difficult to translate, but it reflects violent action against the servant in a court of law. Condemned criminals were not given an honorable burial, and so the servant's grave is with those of the wicked (v. 9). The sufferings of the servant culminate in his death.

The reader learns that the suffering and death of the servant are according to the will of God (vv. 10-12). Behind apparently innocent suffering has stood the purposes of God (see Gen. 50:19-20). Children and long life are to be seen as compensations for the sufferings borne (v. 10). Verse 11 begins with the adversative *waw,* which marks a turning point in the argument. ("The fruit of the travail of his soul" might provide the theme for a sermon that explains how our salvation was won by Christ's suffering on the cross. Salvation and life for believers are the fruits of Christ's travail.)

God is again the speaker (vv. 11-12) who explains that the servant's alternate position with "the great" and "the strong" is because of his outpouring of himself in death. The servant of God grew up unattractively, was alienated from people, suffered for sins he didn't commit, was badly treated in court, put to death, and buried without honor. While we might well ask what it means for God to prosper the servant after he is dead and buried, we are certainly to understand that the servant's history depicts God's judgment on our sin and God's mercy upon us as sinners. God's purpose is to redeem God's people.

For commentary on Gen. 22:1-18, see the Easter Vigil texts to follow.

SECOND LESSON: HEBREWS 4:14-16; 5:7-9; 10:1-25
CHRIST, OUR HIGH PRIEST

The texts from Hebrews may be used to explain theologically the meaning of the events that we will hear narrated from John's Gospel.

The notion of Jesus as High Priest of a new covenant is central to Hebrews (see, for example, 2:17-18; 3:1). Hebrews 4:14—5:10 forms a unit dealing with the priesthood of Jesus.

The point of *Heb. 4:14-16* is that Jesus' own, personal experience qualifies him to be our priest. We are exhorted to hold fast to our faith and to be confident because of Jesus' identification with our condition. Jesus is the "son of God" (v. 14) who has passed from the lesser realms of life to the divine presence. "Our confession" here means our Christian faith. Jesus not only shared our humanity, but he transcended it (v. 15). Because he has shared it, and been tempted, he can sympathize with us. The "throne of grace" (v. 16) suggests that the seat of God is a place of mercy and kindness. God's "throne" speaks to both our past and our future. There we are granted mercy (forgiveness of past sin) and grace (help for our future needs). Here the image of a terrible God of judgment and retribution is superseded by a "compassionate throne room." Because of Christ, we can approach God confidently, sure of God's mercy and grace.

The key term in *Heb. 5:7-9* is obedience. As Jesus was obedient to God (even in suffering), so Christians are to be obedient to the Christ. The author of the passage is obviously deeply moved by the earthly figure of Jesus in his struggle to be obedient. He emphasizes "the days of his flesh" (v. 7), perhaps to underline that Jesus was really human. Verse 7 is frequently taken to be a reference to Jesus' prayer in Gethsemane, and some scholars think the author had a passion narrative available (cf. Mark 14:32-42).

What does it mean to say Jesus "was heard because of his reverent submission"? Prayers heard by God do not necessarily equal requests granted. Jesus was not spared the torment of crucifixion, but was given courage to face it. If God's purposes required allowing the suffering of God's own son, even after hearing Jesus' plea to be spared, can we reasonably expect to escape the suffering common to the human condition? The real test of obedience comes when God's will and our own do not coincide (v. 8; cf. Heb. 12:7-11).

Verse 9 seems to suggest that it was the suffering itself that perfected Jesus. Thus he becomes the source of salvation to all who are obedient to his way of obedience. The writer emphasizes that this salvation is "eternal" or permanent in comparison with that of the High Priests of Judaism, which is temporary and requires at least yearly renewal.

Hebrews 10:1-25 continues in the same vein in explaining how Christ's sacrifice is superior to Temple sacrifice. It describes the futility of repeated animal sacrifice in the light of the eternal efficacy of Christ's sacrifice. Hebrews 10:1-18 demonstrates the superiority of Christ's sacrifice, and the exhortation in 10:19-25 follows from this and works on the basis of typology (comparison of a Hebrew "shadow" with its Christian "reality").

The author passes judgment on the Levitical priesthood (vv. 1-4); they are the "shadow" of which Christ is the reality. This assertion is "proved" (vv. 5-10) by reference to Scripture. Hebrews 5b-7 quotes the LXX version of Ps. 40:6-8 (the key word is "body" in v. 5). The author explains (vv. 8-10) that doing the will of God is more important than sacrifice, a point that was frequently made by Israel's prophets as well.

The priest at the altar is compared with Christ (vv. 11-18), reiterating the point made earlier that Christ is superior. Jeremiah 31:31-34 is quoted in vv. 16-17. If God has forgiven sin to the degree of having forgotten it, sin offerings are no longer needed (v. 18). This leads to a discussion of how people should behave as a result of what Christ has done. (For commentary on this section see the second lesson for Maundy Thursday.)

GOSPEL: JOHN 18:1—19:42
JOHN'S ACCOUNT OF JESUS' PASSION

John's passion narrative follows the Farewell Discourse and High Priestly Prayer of Jesus (chaps. 14–17) and shows the traditional story from a new angle. Throughout, John portrays Jesus as knowing and accepting his fate in the spirit of the self-giving of the footwashing. Because Passover is his theological point of reference, John makes heavy use of Passover imagery like that of the slain lamb, hyssop, blood, and water.

John omits the struggle of Jesus in Gethsemane, and in the arrest (18:1-11) the figure of Jesus stands alone and in sharp relief as he steps out to identify himself. The "I am's" of John come to fulfillment in 18:6 and 8. The garden (18:1) hearkens back to the "beginning" of 1:1 as the new Adam initiates his saving act. The word of fulfillment (18:9) should be compared with 6:39 and 17:12. John individuates response to Jesus by naming Peter (who should have known that carrying a sword at Passover was forbidden) and Malchus (vv. 10-11). In the face of unnecessary force (v. 3), Peter learns that he cannot fight Jesus' battles for him. Shortly, the reader learns the reverse is also true.

By interweaving the accounts of Jesus before the High Priest (18:12-14, 19-24) and Peter's denial (18:15-18, 25-27) John shows Jesus "on trial" both by the religious authorities and by his own. And, ironically, Peter too is on trial. The High Priest, Annas, seeks a charge against Jesus that would carry a capital sentence. The possibilities would include a claim to destroy the Temple, a claim to be the Christ, a prediction of the enthronement of the Son of Man, or blasphemy. In questioning Jesus about his disciples and his teaching (v. 19) Annas may have been concerned about the possibility of an armed uprising. In any case, it was against rabbinic law to try to get evidence from accused persons to incriminate themselves. Jesus' response (v. 21) suggests that he knows this, and it causes the insulting gesture in the following verse. The High Priest seems to be accusing Jesus of being a false teacher and leading others into apostasy; by Deuteronomic law this merited the death penalty.

All four evangelists report "Peter's trial." By means of a disciple who has high priestly connections (v. 15), Peter is brought into the atrium of the house. Only John tells us of the cold night (v. 18). The charcoal fire represents a false light as opposed to the light of the world. In this account Peter refused to confess Jesus, in part, because it would mean the loss of creature comforts and companionship.

Jesus is led from the High Priest to the governor, Caiaphas. Throughout, the focus of his trial is political, revolving around the meaning of *basileus,* king. Jesus' trial before Pilate (18:28—19:16) has three stages. Pilate tries to give Jesus back to be handled by Jewish law. Pilate is reluctant to sentence Jesus in relation to the issue of kingship and proposes to release him as part of a Passover custom. And, finally, Pilate asks Jesus where he is from. In this scene John shows us the real king confronting the apparent authorities. Who is really judge and defendant here?

Note the religious scrupulousness of those who engineer Jesus' death (18:28). Because "evildoer" (v. 30) is not a specific charge, the central question of the trial becomes, "Are you the King of the Jews?" (v. 33). Jesus understands the whole of his life in terms of its final aims; his kingship has to do with what is ultimately true or false (v. 37). In some manuscripts, the crowd calls for "Jesus Barabbas" (v. 40), Jesus,

Son of the Father. The word *robber* (v. 40; Greek, *lestes*) is the word Josephus uses for malcontents, and it introduces political overtones (see Gospel lesson on Mark 11:15-19, Tuesday of Holy Week).

From the time that Jesus is scourged, he is silent except to remind Pilate of the ultimate source of authority (19:11). Pilate seems to use the scourging as an attempt to release Jesus. After the ironic mocking of the true king (19:2-3), the focal point of the trial is reached (v. 5). (One wonders how dangerous the mocked and beaten Jesus can possibly have looked at this point.) The clinching argument with Pilate is political expediency (v. 12), and John tells us that Jesus is "convicted" at exactly the same moment the Passover lambs were being slain (vv. 14-16).

John's account of the crucifixion (19:17-37) has no Simon of Cyrene; Jesus' physical self-sufficiency parallels the spiritual and shows his disciples that they, too, must carry their own crosses. The irony in the crucifixion (v. 18) is intensified when we realize that the center of a group is the place of honor, the place of a king. Verses 19-22 focus again on Jesus' kingship. The casting of lots for Jesus' tunic (which reflects Ps. 22:18) symbolizes both the seamless tunic of the High Priest and the fact that the death of Jesus does not destroy the unity of what he has gathered together.

Verses 26-27 have elicited much commentary, in part because they break the unity of time and space in the passage. Most obviously the text suggests that the church is not to forget the Judaism from which it sprung. (In communities in which anti-Semitism should be addressed this is a good beginning point for the sermon.) Jesus was in control to the very moment of his death (vv. 28-30); for him (and for us) the cross was the means of victory.

Only John relates the piercing of Jesus' side (19:31-37), and, again, his point is to associate Jesus with the Passover lamb. Perhaps he is making an antidocetic statement, showing that Jesus really was flesh, and giving proof of his death. (The insistence on eyewitness accuracy in 19:35 is unique to John.) Blood and water are also highly symbolic in that his followers enter the death of Christ by means of them in Eucharist and baptism. (For reference to blood, see 6:54-56, and water, 4:14.)

The account of the burial of Jesus (19:38-42) suggests that it was to be temporary and that later he was to be moved to a permanent grave. (This would have been standard first-century practice.) Some haste was necessary because this was the "day of preparation," Friday afternoon, and the Sabbath would begin about 6 P.M. We should note the high quality of spice provided by Nicodemus and that Jesus was buried in the same manner as Lazarus (11:44), but the "garden" (v. 41) is peculiar to John (as it was at 18:1). Joseph of Arimathea and Nicodemus laid the body of Jesus in the new tomb temporarily. How temporarily they cannot have known.

Easter Vigil

Lutheran	Roman Catholic	Episcopal	Revised Common
Gen. 1:1—2:3	Gen. 1:1—2:3	Gen. 1:1—2:3	Gen. 1:1—2:4a
Gen. 22:1-18	Gen. 22:1-18	Gen. 22:1-18	Gen. 22:1-18
Exod. 14:10—15:1	Exod. 14:15—15:1	Exod. 14:10—15:1	Exod. 14:10-31; 15:20-21
Isa. 55:1-11	Isa. 55:1-11	Isa. 55:1-11	Isa. 55:1-11
1 Cor. 15:1-11	Rom. 6:3-11	Rom. 6:3-11	Rom. 6:3-11
Luke 24:1-11	Luke 24:1-12	Matt. 28:1-10	Luke 24:1-12

Holy Saturday is usually a day of total fasting. Because of her faith in Jesus' promise to rise again, the day is dedicated to St. Mary. Like the woman at the tomb, the church waits on Holy Saturday.

The earliest references to Pascha (Easter) suggest that it was an evening celebration, probably because the Jewish feast was celebrated at night, but also because the mysteries of darkness and light could be shown to greatest dramatic effect then. Egeria's account of the vigil describes the baptism of catechumens at midnight, the Eucharist, and the reading of the resurrection Gospel.

St. Augustine rightly called the Easter Vigil "the mother of all vigils." On this night the church gathers to celebrate the mystery of the passing from darkness to light and from death to life. Four elements predominate in the liturgies of the Western Church: light (the new fire or paschal candle), water (the baptism of candidates), word (a service of lessons), and bread and cup (the Eucharist).

Traditionally there are twelve lessons appointed for the Easter Vigil, each followed by a prayer and three canticles. Many of the lessons deal with or are types of baptism. The twelve texts summarize salvation history and are catechetical in character and intention. The six lessons chosen for this year's liturgy are drawn from the traditional twelve. Each must be seen in the context of the resurrection of Christ. The problem for the preacher is the richness of these texts and deciding which strand to single out for comment. In most of the selections that follow, detailed commentary is omitted. Instead, themes are suggested that are appropriate to sermons, homilies, or meditations for the vigil.

FIRST LESSON: GENESIS 1:1—2:3 CREATION

This is not the time to introduce the documentary hypothesis, questions about the scientific accuracy of the Bible, or the similarity of Genesis to Babylonian creation myths. The text is best seen as a poetic narrative for liturgical use.

The cosmic meaning of resurrection is highlighted by understanding it in the context of the beginning of creation. Easter has been called "the eighth day of creation," signaling as it does the new creation. The point is that creation has both its origin and its redemption in the will and initiative of God.

The first thing God creates is light. This is easily linked to Jesus' statement, "I am the light of the world," (John 8:12) and to the new fire and paschal candle of the liturgy. The Genesis account glories in the profusion and variety of the creation. Both accounts (Gen. 1:1—2:4a and 2:4b—3:24), culminate in the creation of human beings. Humans are created in the image of God, so that both the male and the female are necessary to complete that image. The likeness, of course, is in the realm of the spirit. Like God, human beings have language and can communicate, have the potential for self-transcendence and, most potently, have the power of creation and procreation. Throughout the text the refrain sounds, "and God saw that it was good." The world and its creatures are valued by God. Against the Greco-Roman paganism of its environment, the Judeo-Christian tradition asserts that the world is good, although tarnished by human *hubris* or overreaching self-assertion. It may be for this reason that the Christian tradition arose which says that the cross was set up on the spot of the tree of life in the Garden of Eden. The cross of Good Friday points the way back to Paradise as the new Adam redeems the sins of the old, or first Adam (see Rom. 5:12-14, 18-19). In the beginning God created the heavens and the earth; in the end God will bring forth the new heaven and the new earth, and that process has begun in the resurrection of Jesus Christ.

SECOND LESSON: GENESIS 22:1-18
THE SACRIFICE OF ISAAC

The first lesson can be linked to the second by noting the fact that the creation, with human beings as its culmination, exists for the purposes of God. This passage is probably the work of the Elohist, with vv. 15-18 a secondary addition. The careful and symmetrical construction of the text should be carefully noted.

The typology that usually comes to mind immediately is the comparison of Isaac with Jesus and Abraham with God. This should not be pushed too far, as the point of the passage is Abraham's radical obedience to God. Because the promise to Abraham rests largely on Isaac, the text holds up the possibility of human faithfulness to God even in the face of extraordinary demands, risks, and losses. And so, in fact, does the crucifixion of Jesus. Abraham is the one who continually risks everything on the faithfulness of God, so perhaps he, and not Isaac, is the Christ parallel (cf. Heb. 11:17-19).

With these thoughts in mind, the sermon or homily might be built around three phrases from the text. "Here I am" (v. 1) speaks of Abraham's obedience. "The fire and the knife" (v. 6) speaks of the cost of obeying God. And "a ram, caught in a thicket" (v. 13) tells of God's provision and intervention, but in God's good time.

It is important to consider the problem of God's "testing of Abraham." William Cooper's turn of phrase, "Behind a frowning providence/He hides a smiling face" is too easy and makes God slightly sadistic. Verse 1 must be taken seriously; God really wants to know something that is settled in v. 12. This episode is not a game with God. It is deadly serious for Abraham.

Finally, then, in Abraham's painful obedience we see an important lesson. When human love is lifted above possessive particularity, and the beloved is freely given to God's purposes (and yet remains beloved), human life itself shows forth its divine origin, and is ultimately redeemed.

For particularly helpful commentary on the first two lessons the preacher might consult Walter Brueggemann's *Genesis* in the Interpretation Commentary Series (Atlanta: John Knox Press, 1982).

THIRD LESSON: EXODUS 14:10—15:1
CROSSING THE RED SEA

The Red Sea text ends the first third of the traditional twelve-part vigil service. Deliverance at the Red Sea is the root experience of Israel's faith, representing the means by which God brought them together as a people.

There are many connections to the sacrifice of Isaac. In both stories God comes through, seemingly at the last moment, to redeem his own in extremis (see 1 Cor. 10:13). Here, however, Israel is not delivered because of her faith, but in spite of the lack thereof, as the faith of Moses is contrasted with the fear of the people. In both texts, salvation rests on God's initiative.

God, who is the source of redemption, uses both divine and ordinary means in the Red Sea episode: an angel of God and a pillar of cloud, the hand of Moses and a strong east wind, God and the mud. Even extraordinary deliverances can come through commonplace events and people.

An interesting homily could be built around verses 13 and 31: "Do not be afraid, stand firm, and see the deliverance that the LORD will accomplish for you today" and "Israel saw . . . and believed." For some, at least, it is seeing that leads to believing. This is what John tells us of the disciple whom Jesus loved at the empty tomb; "He saw and believed" (John 20:8).

The problem to be addressed in this passage is that of a childish faith, which would assert that God always intervenes on behalf of the "good guys." Those who lived through the Nazi years in Europe, who know of the circumstances of the Normandy invasion on D day, who survived the Holocaust, or who understand the plight of the Palestinian people will find that such an assertion falls flat. God's deliverance and God's silence and seeming inactivity must both be lifted up.

Finally, the Red Sea episode has long been understood in Christian tradition as a type of baptism (see, for example, 1 Cor. 10:1-13). In the New Testament, Jesus is the fulfillment of the exodus. The first exodus, followed as it was by the giving of the law on Mt. Sinai, was inadequate to bring about God's plan and goal. The deliverance effected by Jesus' death and resurrection is complete, as the great baptismal text in Romans 6 (which shall be discussed shortly) so clearly declares.

FOURTH LESSON: ISAIAH 55:1-11 "COME TO THE WATERS"

Traditionally Isa. 55:1-11 opens the second part of the Easter Vigil, with its four lessons from the prophets. In Deutero-Isaiah the text is a hymn celebrating the coming redemption of Israel. It is the last prophecy in Deutero-Isaiah and brings that work to a triumphant close. Note that God is the speaker throughout, except in vv. 6-7, which is a call by the prophet to seek God and to abandon sin.

The gifts of the new and everlasting covenant are symbolized by lifegiving food and drink (vv. 1-2). The literary form is reminiscent of Prov. 9:1-6, wisdom's invitation to a banquet. Here, the call to a banquet is a call to life (and the parallel to the Eucharist is obvious). Royal covenant theology promises that the lineage of David will reign forever (vv. 3-5). Note that the promise is because of "the Lord your God" (v. 5), and not the result of anything David, or any human, has done.

God is near and the time of deliverance is at hand (vv. 6-11). Ezekiel 18:25-29 provides an interesting commentary (vv. 8-9). Perhaps attention to the "word" (vv. 10-11) is the richest source for preaching. Recall, first, that in Hebrew "word" and "deed" are expressed by a single word, and, second, that in the Genesis account God created by means of the word. Rain, the point of comparison with "word," is considered by the ancient Mesopotamian religions as the greatest gift of the gods. "Word" is especially potent for its New Testament associations, both with the person of Christ and Scripture, generally. Note the absolute conviction (v. 11).

Literary analysis of the text reveals that it is made up of five strophes, the first three of which contain urgent imperatives. Perhaps the germ of the sermon is found in those verbs: *come, buy, eat, listen, delight, seek, call, forsake, return.* Where we go, what we buy, eat, delight in, listen to, and seek tells a great deal about us. Whom do we call upon? What must we forsake? To whom do we return? And what light does the resurrection of Jesus shed on the answers to these questions?

The context of the resurrection also points up the three great theological themes of the passage and their connection to the previous lessons. They are, first, the inscrutability of God's ways (here vv. 8-9 and the Abraham and Isaac story); second, the universality of God's generosity (v. 1) and grace (v. 7; with its parallel in creation itself); and, third, the inevitability of the accomplishment of God's will (here vv. 10-11, evident in the crossing of the Red Sea).

FIFTH LESSON: ROMANS 6:3-11
BAPTIZED INTO CHRIST JESUS

Careful treatment of the epistle is especially important if baptisms are to be part of the Easter Vigil. The text links the great spiritual themes of night-death and baptism-resurrection, and expresses the cosmic meaning of the resurrection of Jesus in the life of the believer. The metaphor on which the passage depends is dramatic and visual and works only when baptism (from Greek, *baptizo,* "to dip") is understood as immersion. (Note the important and repeated comparison in vv. 3, 4a, 5a, 8a of buried or died with Christ.)

Chapters 5–8 may be the most important in the Roman letter, as they treat "new life" in Christ. Our text occurs in the section on sin and law (6:1—7:25). The ground has been laid for the series of rhetorical questions that open chapter 6 in 5:12-21. Paul is responding to those who think his "freedom from law" inevitably means "freedom for sin." (Is he responding to antinomians in Rome?)

It may be that in the phrase "baptized into Christ Jesus" (v. 3), Jesus is to be understood as a composite personality, that of the new and redeemed humanity, of which he is the Head. Thus, to be baptized into Christ is to be incorporated into the body of Christ. Baptism is absolutely crucial (v. 4; this is the first instance of the metaphor by which immersion is compared to burial); by baptism the believer receives "new life." Note, however, that "walking" in that new life requires a certain effort.

The construction of v. 5 is obscure, but it points to the fact that resurrection presupposes death. The word for "united" (Greek, *sumphutoi*) means literally "grown together" and is an image of grafting (an image that Paul will use to good effect in Romans 11). Just as walking in newness of life requires effort, loss of the old self is at some cost (v. 6). Death with Christ is in some measure an ethical experience (v. 7). The literal point is that the dead are no longer in a position to rebel against God. Verse 8 may reflect an early confession of faith. In substance, it echoes and reinforces v. 4. Death with Christ has already occurred in baptism; however, "will . . . live" is something in the future. Participation in Christ's death is in the past tense; participation in his resurrection is in the future.

Verses 9 and 10 are the great Easter affirmation and the heart of its message. "Death no longer has dominion"; that is, death can no longer "lord over" or rule over; *kurievei* suggests the idea of a master-slave relationship. That relationship is severed in the resurrection of Christ. His death was completely sufficient, and his resurrection was an eschatological event of the first order. Paul therefore admonishes his hearers, "you also must consider yourselves dead to sin and alive to

God in Christ Jesus." This admonition (v. 11) is the reason for the discussion of baptism (cf. Gal. 5:24). The baptized person may not look different, but he or she is now related to God in a completely new way. Baptism is (in part) that public affirmation of trust in the new possibilities of life that Christ has opened. It is both a community event and the point of the individual's absolute identification with Jesus Christ and his aims and purposes.

Seen in the context of the Easter Vigil, Rom. 6:3-11 is a vivid reminder of how each individual Christian in some small measure mirrors the experiences of his or her Lord. We, too, must die and be raised to new life. Our resurrection presupposes our death, but because of Jesus' prior activity, that death no longer has mastery. The closing words of John Donne's sonnet, "Death, thou shalt die," are not quite accurate. Death has already died.

LUTHERAN FIFTH LESSON: 1 CORINTHIANS 15:1-11
THE CHURCH'S PROCLAMATION

On the night of the resurrection it is appropriate that the church be reminded of the earliest and most basic summary of its proclamation or kerygma. Following a long discussion of propriety in worship (11:2—14:40), Paul reminds the Corinthian church of the four elements of the Christian kerygma, stressing that Jesus' resurrection is "proved" both by Scripture and by witnesses. This is important because some at Corinth had apparently denied the resurrection (see 15:12).

Paul's gospel (like that of Peter's as reflected in the Pentecost sermon in Acts 2) has as its basic focus the death and resurrection of Jesus. That message is summarized here as a preface to a discussion of resurrection from the dead in general (vv. 12-34) and of the form in which persons are resurrected (vv. 38-57).

Paul reminds the Corinthians (vv. 1-2) that this summary of the gospel brings together the past (I preached and you received), the present (you stand), and the future (you are saved, continuous action). Verse 3 is a technical formula in Paul for the handing on of tradition (see 1 Cor. 11:23). "As of first importance" may be an addition to the original text. "First" (Greek, *protos*) can mean priority of time or of importance.

The four points of the early kerygma, then, are as follows: First, Christ died for sins according to Scripture (v. 3). The reference in question is probably Isa. 53:5-12 (see first lesson for Good Friday) and the fact that the death was "in accordance with the scriptures" establishes the continuity of salvation history and reminds them of God's sovereignty over history. Second, Christ was buried (v. 4). This is understood as the proof that he really died. Third, Christ was raised on the third day according to Scripture (v. 4; cf. Ps. 16:10). Here the "in accordance with the scriptures" may allude to the fact that resurrection was a common expectation.

Resurrection was certainly a tenet of Pharisaic Judaism (Acts 23:6-10) and Paul was, himself, a Pharisee (Phil. 3:5). Resurrection itself may have been a common expectation, but the specific resurrection of Jesus was a complete surprise as all four Gospel accounts attest. "Was raised," the perfect indicative passive of *egeiro* in Greek, indicates that Jesus was the object of the action. God raised him; thus, his resurrection is proof of the claims about him. Furthermore, the perfect indicates a continuing condition; Christ continues in the resurrected form and has introduced the possibility of a new condition for humanity. Finally, this risen Christ appeared to witnesses (vv. 5-8), which is part of the proof that he was really alive again.

Note that the risen Christ appeared to the Twelve (v. 5) and to the apostles (v. 7). This suggests that the two groups were not synonymous. Acts mentions at least one apostle not of the Twelve (Barnabas) and Romans names a female apostle, one Junia (Rom. 16:7). (See "Junia . . . Outstanding among the Apostles" by Bernadette Brooten and "The Twelve" by Elisabeth Schüssler Fiorenza, in Leonard & Arlene Swidler, eds., *Women Priests* [New York: Paulist Press, 1977].)

GOSPEL: LUKE 24:1-12
WHY SEEK THE LIVING AMONG THE DEAD?

The Lukan account of the resurrection focuses on the experience of the women. The way the story is written gives their experience of the empty tomb priority over what the two men (angels?) say. It is not insignificant that in all four Gospel accounts of the empty tomb the experience of the faithful women is the beginning point of the proclamation of Jesus' resurrection. (As a result, in the Orthodox tradition St. Mary Magdalene is treated as an apostle.)

The women come on the first day of the week, after the Jewish Sabbath (cf. Luke 23:54-56 to give continuity to the story), literally at "deep dawn" (Greek, *orthrou batheos*). The fact that they are bringing the spices they had prepared (on the Sabbath, thus having understood Jesus' teaching on the Sabbath?) suggests they were not expecting the resurrection. The tomb was of a form common at that time, a rolling stone tomb. Hollowed out of a small cave or in a rock wall, the tomb entrance was closed by a stone that rolled back and forth in a groove. Upon entering such a tomb one comes into a larger preparation area (sometimes with a trench in the floor in which those preparing the bodies stood) where bodies were made ready to be placed in smaller niches hollowed out at the back of the preparation room. Jesus' body was undoubtedly placed hastily in this preparation area awaiting proper ministrations before it was finally to be inserted into one of the niches for permanent burial. The fact that the women went into the burial cave is evidence (if more is needed!) of their courage.

Luke plays on what was and was not "found." They "found the stone rolled away" (v. 2), but they "did not find the body" (v. 3). They had seen the tomb and how the body was laid (23:55), so their surprise is understandable. "Two men in dazzling clothes stood by them" (v. 4). "Stood" does not capture the sense of *epestesav,* which means "to come upon suddenly or unexpectedly, to burst upon." The women's physical courage is again attested in that they are not afraid until the men appear (v. 5); then they prostrate themselves (perhaps because they know they are in the presence of angels).

The message of the angels (vv. 5b-7) begins with the great existential question of Easter: Why seek the living among the dead? The women are asked to recall that Jesus had told them all that would happen, and, of course, they have been with Jesus throughout the ministry (see Luke 8:1-3). The verbs (v. 7) *handed over, crucified,* and *rise,* summarize the kerygma in much the same terms as 1 Cor. 15:1-11 (see above).

The simplicity of v. 8 is deceptive. "They remembered" implies that all that Jesus taught and said suddenly comes into sharp and penetrating focus in the women's minds. And so they return immediately to tell the others, thereby becoming the first evangelists of the resurrection and demonstrating how the logical outcome of any experience of resurrection is proclamation. When the dead rise, there is news to be shared! Verse 10 is important to Luke's methodology as outlined in 1:1-4. These particular women have been with Jesus since the beginning of his ministry (8:1-3); they saw him die (23:49); and watched as the body was placed in the tomb (23:55). They are credible witnesses of the resurrection. That fact makes the apostles' disbelief even more poignant (v. 11). "The eleven and the rest" (v. 9), the men, do not believe what the women report. Worse, they count it *loros,* idle talk or nonsense, in the medical terminology of the time, the talk of the sick in delirium. Because it is delivered by women (who, of course, under the circumstances would be "emotional" and "irrational"!), the message of the resurrection is at first discounted. How often has crucial, indeed, life-changing information been ignored or rejected because it was delivered by those of the wrong sex, color, nationality, religion, or socioeconomic group?

Verse 12 is omitted from many important ancient manuscripts, notably Bezae and O. L. MSS. Many scholars suggest it is an addition to Luke's text based on John 20:3-10 and is intended to "rehabilitate" Peter, or at least to show him in a somewhat brighter light than the other male disciples (vv. 9 and 11).

The experience of the women provides us with a paradigm for the Christian life. The very worst had happened to them. The one who had raised their status, accepted them into the rabbinic circle, and had such promise was lost. Even in their confusion, pain, and grief they carry out the duties expected of them, and in the process of "doing their duty," a remarkable thing happens. They are recalled to themselves (much as Mary is recalled to herself by the voice of the Master in John 20:16). Having experienced the glorious reality of the resurrection, they return to their ordinary situation and companions with an extraordinary message. And they are hardly greeted with enthusiasm! Even the wonderful resurrection message is not sugarcoated, but strikes a note of reality. The resurrections of our lives may not be greeted with joy, or even accepted, by those with whom we journey. This does not excuse us from following the basic pattern set by Mary Magdalene, Joanna, and Mary: to go, to remember, to return, to tell.

EPISCOPAL GOSPEL: MATTHEW 28:1-10
REJOICE! DO NOT BE AFRAID!

The preacher need not worry about harmonizing the various accounts of the empty tomb. Easter faith is based on a risen Lord, not an empty tomb. Matthew's account is substantially an expansion of the shorter ending of Mark (16:1-8) and focuses on the message of the angel and the words of Jesus rather than the experience of the women who, however, are again the first to see the empty tomb and the risen Lord.

In Matthew, the women are going to "see the sepulchre" (v. 1) (because the body has already been prepared for burial; 27:59-60?). Matthew's earthquake signals a theophany and is in keeping with his tendency to allude to, if not outright quote, Hebrew Scripture. Here the angel is the agent of the stone's removal. That angel (v. 3) is Matthew's explanation of the "young man in white" in Mark 16:5, and fear of him has rendered the guards (set by the chief priests and Pharisees who seem to have been expecting trouble; 27:62-66), powerless.

The angel begins his message to the women (vv. 5-7) begins, as well he might, by telling them not to be afraid. As an angelic being, he has prescience of their reason for being at the tomb. The Jesus they seek is no longer in the tomb. The proof that he is risen is that his body is not where they saw it laid, not where Joseph of Arimathea put it (27:57-61). The angel commissions the women to tell the disciples that Jesus is risen and is going to meet them in Galilee, the locus of their normal, ordinary lives and activity. Jesus is to be seen in the usual, domestic round.

The women leave with "fear and great joy" (v. 8). The fear is accounted for when we recall that resurrections from the dead would have been understood at the time as a sign of the end of the age (Matthew has already suggested this idea in 27:51-53). Joy is the human response to having discovered that an apparently lost beloved has been returned. As they run to tell the disciples, Jesus himself meets them. His message is substantially the same as that of the angel. But his first word to them is not, "do not be afraid," but "Greetings!" or "rejoice" (Greek, *chairete*). The evil powers of this world, in the guise of politics or of religion, have done their worst, but God has triumphed. Jesus has "conquered the world" (John 16:33).

Again, Jesus charges the women to tell the believers to go to Galilee. "There they will see me" (v. 10). Jesus certainly will not be encountered in the cemeteries and tombs of life, in the past, in the might-have-beens. Nor is he always to be found in the earthquake and lightning of an Easter morning, empty tomb experience. Both the angel of the resurrection and the resurrected Christ suggest that he is to be found in our own, personal Galilees, in the ordinary walk of our daily round. It is in "Galilee," thus understood, that we are commanded to rejoice and to be unafraid. He is risen. He "goes before us" here and now. This is the message that we must go quickly and tell.